Praise for *Pow*

Powerful Questioning is going t
who reads it. Chiles brillian
strategies to unpick the subtle
classroom. It can be too easy to take questioning for granted, so
common is it to the classroom, but for even experienced teachers,
it can prove a tricky aspect of teaching to improve. This book offers
a wealth of useful reflection, along with activities and insights, to
propel teachers' questioning skills towards expert levels.

**Alex Quigley, author of *Closing the Writing Gap*, National Content
and Engagement Manager, Education Endowment Foundation**

Questioning is possibly the most powerful lever teachers have
in the classroom to drive learning. This book is an authoritative
work not just on the research underpinning it but also on how to
use it in practice. Highly recommended.

Dr Carl Hendrick, co-author of *How Learning Happens*

Some salutary statistics here on the range of questions currently
asked in our classrooms and the massive opportunities for deepening pupils' learning when we reconsider how to extract best
value from them. Michael Chiles has written a terrific book to
explain why and to show us how. An essential resource for CPD
for every school.

Mary Myatt, education writer, speaker and curator, Myatt & Co

One can't help but marvel at how Michael has been able to weave
important research with his classroom insight to make this book on
questioning a valuable contribution to every teacher's professional
learning. 'Questions are an integral part of our daily lives', Michael
asserts, and I tend to think this book will be an integral part of
developing our essential question-asking skills in the classroom.

**Dr Steven Berryman, President, Chartered College of
Teaching, Director of Creativity, Music and Culture,
Charter Schools Educational Trust**

The best teachers ask lots of questions. But what are the most effective questions to ask? When and how should we ask them? And how can we shape our classroom environment so that students feel comfortable answering questions?

In this impressive book, Michael Chiles provides compelling answers to these key questions and more. *Powerful Questioning* expertly deconstructs the art of questioning, offering highly practical advice for every classroom practitioner.

**Mark Roberts, English teacher, Director of Research,
Carrickfergus Grammar School**

At the heart of every great lesson is questioning. Yet, for years, the CPD around questioning had been limited to simply 'closed questions are bad' and 'open questions are good'. If we were lucky, then someone might even waft Bloom's taxonomy to spice things up or the facilitator might get you to throw questions scrunched into paper balls or pass questions around on Post-it notes, because it was done once in an 'Outstanding' lesson.

Micheal Chiles' *Powerful Questioning* is a thoughtful and thorough exploration of how to effectively use questioning in the classroom. Rather than looking at fancy tricks, Chiles explores the creation, use, function and impact of questions in education. The narrow focus really helps you to refine and question your existing practice. As the title suggests, questioning can be powerful and we, as practitioners, need to explore and consider how we can make every interaction have an impact in the classroom.

A book that proves that you can teach an old dog, like me, a few tricks and, of course, there's loads of stuff for new dogs, I mean teachers, too.

**Chris Curtis, Head of English, author of *How to Teach
English: Novels, Non-Fiction and their Art of Navigation***

Michael Chiles states in *Powerful Questioning*, 'of all the pedagogy strategies at the teacher's disposal, questioning is one of the most dominant methods of instruction. It is the heartbeat of a classroom.' I found this to be true in my years of working with cognitive scientists researching how children learn in a classroom. In my experience, questioning is fundamental in pursuing the powerful tools of retrieval, spacing, interleaving and metacognition, all rooted in robust research. Understanding how we learn and using the proper questioning techniques that develop critical thinking assists the teacher in promoting successful learning. John Hattie states in the introduction, 'The hard part is asking the right question at the right time for the right purpose and with the right level of complexity.' Michael Chiles gives us the knowledge and techniques that will make our use of questioning most effective.

Patrice M. Bain, co-author of *Powerful Teaching: Unleash the Science of Learning* and *Organizing Instruction and Study to Improve Student Learning*, author of *A Parent's Guide to Powerful Teaching*

Teachers ask hundreds of questions a day in their classrooms. But do we make the most of them? In this superbly researched and referenced book, Michael Chiles explores the purpose and untapped potential of questioning within classroom pedagogy, giving the reader powerful insight into this crucial element of effective teaching. As well as examining why questioning matters for responsive teaching, he carefully dissects the types of questioning we can use but also how questions can be used in formative assessment to check for understanding, diagnose and support pupil reflection. His approach is carefully interwoven with cognitive science and how questioning can support both deeper thinking and the long-term acquisition of knowledge and skills. He doesn't duck the fact that both teachers and pupils can often find questioning hard; rather, he explores the reasons behind these challenges and offers practical and accessible strategies that can build classroom culture to allow powerful questioning to flourish and thrive. As with his previous books on assessment and feedback, this book is another gem – rooted in his own rich personal reflections and experience, his passion for teaching and his love of learning more about what makes the biggest difference in classrooms and to pupils' success. A must-read for teachers and leaders in all settings.

Andy Buck, Founder of Leadership Matters and BASIC Coaching

Effective questioning techniques and strategies to promote deep thinking are crucial aspects of an effective teacher's classroom toolkit. In this book, Michael Chiles provides a plethora of examples underpinned by research to elicit our own deep thinking of how and why we ask questions in our classrooms. Within each chapter there are multiple reflection tasks and related activities for readers to complete, making this book not just something to read but, more importantly, something to practise. A superb addition to any classroom teacher's pedagogical bookcase.

Jon Tait, education leader, author and speaker

Powerful. Questioning

Strategies for Improving Learning and Retention in the Classroom

Michael Chiles

Crown House Publishing Limited
www.crownhouse.co.uk

First published by

Crown House Publishing Ltd
Crown Buildings, Bancyfelin, Carmarthen, Wales, SA33 5ND, UK
www.crownhouse.co.uk

and

Crown House Publishing Company LLC
PO Box 2223
Williston, VT 05495, USA
www.crownhousepublishing.com

British Library of Cataloguing-in-Publication Data
A catalogue entry for this book is available from the British Library.

Print ISBN: 978-178583596-4
Mobi ISBN: 978-178583676-3
ePub ISBN: 978-178583677-0
ePDF ISBN: 978-178583678-7

LCCN 2022950664

Printed in the UK by
Gomer Press, Llandysul, Ceredigion

Foreword by John Hattie

My 3-year-old granddaughters are deep into the 'why' questions, as they try to understand their world, build a theory of mind and express their curiosity. By age 8 they will have switched to asking 'what' questions, and so often lose their innate sense of wonder, mimic their teachers and aim to be compliant so as to be a 'good pupil'. As teenagers they are more likely to ask 'why not', as their development of autonomy clashes with the school and often family desire for compliance, and as young adults they switch to 'how much'. If only it were this simple, if only we could retain all these forms of questions, and if only we considered questions as about more than seeking answers but inviting thinking. If only we saw errors to questions not as sources of embarrassment but as opportunities for learning.

We humans love to ask other questions, seek answers and contemplate next questions. We see questioning as a core to seeking wisdom, and cite Socrates' methods for eliciting ideas, promoting connections and showing that the answers were always there just waiting to emerge. There are so many books on how to ask great questions, we can become absorbed in TV shows like *Jeopardy!* and *Mastermind*, and we can also have 'the' question we want to ask politicians, famous people or gurus. That is the easy part.

The hard part is asking the right question at the right time for the right purpose and with the right level of complexity. As educators, we spend so much time on devising the right question when our aim may be more about eliciting the right response – maybe inviting pupils to contemplate, use learning strategies to come to the right answer, work with others to prioritise the optimal answer or to draw out wrong answers so as to better understand how they are thinking. What an unusual profession where the purpose of questioning is not simply to get the right answer!

There have been many studies showing that the dominant mode of class questions is the IRE cycle: *initiate* a question, get a *response* and the teacher *evaluates* the response. The reason for so much questioning relates to the mind frames about teaching and learning held by many teachers – that is, their role is to impart knowledge and information about a subject, and pupil learning is the acquisition of this information through the processes of repetition, memorisation and recall. Hence, the need for much questioning to check they have recalled this information. Teachers can dominate the class regarding questions, and questions are the second most common teaching method after teacher talk. The estimates of teacher questions vary between 100 and 350 a day, and the responses from these questions are typically some form of recall of facts, judgement or correction, primarily reinforcing, affirming, restating and consolidating pupil responses.

Teachers already know the answer to over 80% of the questions they ask, most of the questions are closed, with low cognitive demands on pupils, and the typical question requires less than a three-word answer. Not all questions are the same or have the same impact. Throughout *Powerful Questioning*, the many types of questions are explored, and the aim is to move past the IRE schedule.

There have been nine meta-analyses (no. studies = 270) of the effects of questioning on achievement with an overall effect size of 0.51, and seven meta-analyses (no. studies = 360) of pupil self-questioning with an overall effect size of 0.53. Imagine the effect size if we moved beyond the factual, the accurate, the IRE schedule. Here is where this book is so powerful.

Teachers can hear their impact from the answers to their questions, but more so when they hear the pupils' questions. How many questions about their thinking and ponderings do we hear in a day (about two!)? So often, pupils want to ask, 'Why is this so?' whereas we ask, 'What is so?' but perhaps it is no surprise that so many pupil questions in class mimic our use of the IRE schedule, expecting a less than three-word answer by the teacher and thus missing a richness and the skills required for our pupils to engage in asking more impactful questions. As Michael Chiles quotes, 'The greatest attribute of questioning is that it stimulates thinking in the classroom,' and questioning is 'the single most influential teaching act' because questions empower pupils to think, which in turn can contribute towards enhancing learning – so we had better get it right. Surely, our aim is not to develop quiz-kids filled with facts, three-word or fewer answerers or to ask questions to which they already know the answer.

Questions can vary from lower to higher order, and getting the balance right at the right time to the right level of complexity is a major purpose of *Powerful Questioning*. Michael Chiles documents the various purposes of questions and pushes us to move beyond checking the facts and knowledge status of pupils (usually a select group) in the class, and to use questions to activate thinking, promote reflection and pose challenges. Questions can inform the teacher of their impact, lead to different directions in the lesson and invite joint teacher–pupil investigation of answers. He investigates the ways to build a questioning culture by increasing pupil questions and explains beautifully how to use questions so pupils can check for understanding, to move from lower to higher order questions (and back again), to assess progress towards success criteria and how pupils can effectively question each other to build pupil collective efficacy about their learning.

Video your teaching before and after reading this book, and note the switch from IRE dominance to sharing the questioning with the pupils, and noting how the pupils become more engaged in the learning when they take the role of questioners.

John Hattie

Acknowledgements

A huge thank you to John Hattie for sharing his reflections on questioning and writing the foreword. Thanks also to the contributors who shared their thoughts on the power of questioning in education, as well as all the teachers I have observed over the years. You are an inspiration for the next generation of teachers and make a difference to pupils' lives every day.

I would also like to extend my gratitude to the Great Schools Trust, in particular Shane Ierston and Katie Sharp for their support while I was writing the book.

Finally, thank you to my wife, Sarah Thornton.

Contents

Introduction

The power of a question

> The greatest attribute of questioning is that it stimulates thinking in the classroom.
>
> **Michele Filippone[1]**

Questioning is a staple feature of a teacher's toolkit across all phases of education. Our classrooms are awash with explanation, modelling and feedback, but of all the pedagogy strategies at the teacher's disposal, questioning is one of the most dominant methods of instruction. It is the heartbeat of a classroom.

Take a moment to consider the last lesson you taught and how many questions you asked. Teachers are described by many as 'professional question-askers', and the use of questioning in the teaching and learning process dates back to one of the most influential users and developers of questions, the Greek philosopher Socrates. Socrates believed that by asking questions we encourage reflection, and their use is most effective when we create a continual loop of dialogue between the asker and the receiver, to allow movement from surface to deeper level thinking. Questions are the tool that enable teachers to transfer knowledge, leading to the conclusion that effective questioning is effective teaching.

Classroom teachers worldwide spend a large percentage of their time in the questioning–response mode; so much so that several

---

1   M. Filippone, Questioning at the Elementary Level. Unpublished MA dissertation, Kean University, NJ (1998), p. 7. Available at: https://eric.ed.gov/?id=ED417431.

research studies indicate that an estimated 40% of classroom time is spent in this mode.[2] Therefore, we can deduce that questioning must be a pivotal element in the teaching and learning process, and that asking good questions plays a critical part in supporting pupil achievement. The time spent questioning has remained fairly consistent since 1912, with Leven and Long identifying that 8% of the school day is spent asking questions – a statistic that remained static between 1912 and 1981.[3]

With all this time spent asking questions, we might assume that most teachers in most classrooms encourage pupils to think with the questions they ask. However, while questioning is a dominant component of many lessons across all phases, Orletsky indicated that all too often the questions teachers ask haven't been well prepared and don't serve the purpose of encouraging pupils to think.[4] Therefore, the art of asking questions is masked by the purpose of the questions asked, leaving a gap between question delivery and its subsequent impact on pupil achievement.

> **Pedagogy reflection:** Taking our time to create purposeful questions will be more beneficial than merely asking lots of purposeless questions.

The art of asking questions underpins everything we do as teachers. It is the backbone of communication between teachers and pupils, pupils and pupils, and teachers and teachers. As Filippone noted in the epigraph at the beginning of the chapter, it 'stimulates thinking' to encourage reflection and initiate information recall, which in turn reveals the quality of what pupils are thinking and

2   J. H. Johnston, G. C. Markle and A. Hayley-Oliphant, What Research Says About Questioning in the Classroom, *Middle School Journal*, 18(4) (1987), 29–33.
3   T. Leven and R. Long, *Effective Instruction* (Washington, DC: Association for Supervision and Curriculum Development, 1981).
4   S. Orletsky, *Questioning and Understanding to Improve Learning and Thinking (QUILT): The Evaluation Results* (Charleston, WV: Appalachia Educational Laboratory, 1997). Available at: https://eric.ed.gov/?id=ED403230.

their degree of understanding. It is the key to unlocking what is hidden, the fuel to prompt further thought and the shining light to developing a deeper understanding. This is reinforced by Ausubel who said: 'The most important single factor influencing learning is what the learner already knows. Ascertain this and teach him/her accordingly.'[5]

Without questions, we are essentially left in the dark about what our pupils know and don't know. As Ausubel observed, we need to ascertain what learners already know in order to decide what needs to be taught. We do this by asking questions. Without knowing what our pupils have learned, we can't support them to move forward and develop their understanding further. In fact, its role as a teaching tool in the classroom has been the subject of studies for many years, which alongside my own personal experiences and that of other practising teachers will underpin a lot of the discussion that threads throughout the book. As with any research, it isn't a one-size-fits-all approach, meaning that the research outlined and the strategies suggested for you to use in your classroom, or as a leader to introduce to colleagues, might look different to fit your context. We certainly can't adopt a tick-box culture when using questions as a pedagogic tool in our classrooms. What we can do is examine the best bets from the research and consider how they might apply with the pupils we support in our own communities, as well as the colleagues with whom we work.

That is the reason why, alongside unravelling the reasons behind why we ask questions as well as the potential power of asking questions, I will also outline a set of core principles, recommendations and classroom-based scenarios that can be used to implement powerful questioning in your classroom and school. After fifteen years of teaching, I am a firm believer that creating a set of key principles for pedagogy, such as how schools approach giving feedback or using assessment to judge pupil performance, is beneficial

....

5   D. P. Ausubel, *Educational Psychology: A Cognitive View* (New York: Holt, Rinehart & Winston), cited in E. C. Wragg and G. Brown, *Questioning in the Secondary School* (Successful Teaching Series) (London: Routledge, 2001), p. 7.

because it reduces the potential for a tick-list approach to applying research in the classroom. When this happens, school leaders tend to use the same blanket approach across all phases and subjects.

Let's look at one example to illustrate this. One of the main findings I have taken from reading over sixty research papers on questioning is that the most effective teachers ask lots of questions in their classrooms. At face value, this is a true statement. However, quantity is a poor proxy for quality if what we want is for teachers to ask powerful questions that generate more than surface-level thinking. It would miss what we have started to unravel in this introduction, that the intention and delivery of the question is more important than the number of questions asked. Gall emphasised the importance of asking quality questions, commenting that it is the quality rather than the quantity of teacher questions that promotes pupil learning.[6] In my experience, the tick-list approach to implementing pedagogy in schools isn't effective and ultimately has a negative impact on learning.

With this in mind, as you engage with the content in the book, there will be opportunities to spend some time reflecting on your own practice and experience of asking questions with a series of activities that you can complete either by yourself or with colleagues in your department. This feels like an ideal moment to begin with our first activity.

6   M. D. Gall, The Use of Questions in Teaching, *Review of Educational Research*, 40(5) (1970), 707–721. https://doi.org/10.3102/00346543040005707

Activity

Research-based evidence is now a common feature within schools. Thinking about your own school context, what research-based pedagogy strategies have been introduced recently? Do you feel you have had time to implement the strategies within the context of your subject?

If yes, can you identify the mechanisms used to implement the strategy?

If no, what factors do you think might have affected its implementation?

When teachers use questions, it opens the door to establishing to what extent their explanations and models have been understood, it allows pupils to express their views and develop their understanding of a subject, and it provides teachers and pupils with opportunities to give feedback. So compelling is this view that curriculum reformer and teacher-educator Hilda Taba declared that when teachers use questions it is 'the single most influential teaching act'[7] because when they are used to prompt pupils to think deeply about knowledge, they have the potential to contribute towards enhancing learning.

A teacher could end up asking over a million questions over the course of their career.[8] These will vary from lower to higher order questions, promoting surface to deeper level thinking depending on the type and number of questions asked. Getting this balance right is challenging, and it seems that the research is inconclusive on which of these types of questions is more effective. However, I

---

7   H. Taba, *Teaching Strategies and Cognitive Functioning in Elementary School Children*. Cooperative Research Project No. 2404 (San Francisco, CA: San Francisco State College, 1966), cited in W. W. Wilen (ed.), *Questions, Questioning Techniques, and Effective Teaching* (Washington, DC: National Education Association, 1987), p. 14. Available at: https://files.eric.ed.gov/fulltext/ED310102.pdf.
8   Wragg and Brown, *Questioning in the Secondary School*, p. vii.

will outline how combining these different questions strategically using a linear approach is more likely to create the foundations for developing and deepening pupil understanding. It is a bit like constructing a tower: you need a strong base on which to build the columns and to create the stability necessary to add increasing numbers of floors and height to the building. When asking questions, we need to start with those that elicit initial recall and then move towards those that prompt deeper thinking, requiring pupils to do some deep excavation from stored memories in their schema to articulate their understanding in new or unfamiliar contexts.

Schemas enable us to form a mental representation of the world. The term was first introduced by Jean Piaget who believed that schema underpinned key stages in cognitive development. Piaget defined schema as 'a cohesive, repeatable action sequence possessing component actions that are tightly interconnected and governed by core meaning'.[9] From Piaget's definition, we can summarise that a schema is a way to organise knowledge in 'files' that relate to different aspects of the world. As a person develops, so the number and complexity of schemas increase. In essence, neither lower order nor higher order questions are necessarily better than the other, but a combination of both in the question–response mode have the power to assist in stimulating thinking and building a more advanced understanding of the world around us. We will explore this further in Chapter 3.

Pedagogy reflection: Combining the use of lower order and higher order questions will be more powerful than using them in isolation.

Right from the beginning, trainee teachers will be asking hundreds of different types of question as they develop their craft

---

9   J. Piaget, *The Origins of Intelligence in Children*, tr. M. T. Cook (New York: International Universities Press, 1952), p. 7.

in the classroom. Many of these questions will be fired at pupils with the aim of checking for understanding, activating thinking, recalling knowledge, promoting reflection, reinforcing expectation and posing a challenge.

In a research study of forty teachers, Brown and Edmondson found that the most common criteria teachers cited for asking questions was pupils' ability, with the main reasons including: for gaining attention and understanding (high ability), for checking and revision (medium ability) and for understanding and management (low ability).[10] The reasons and percentages are listed below, with encouraging thought, checking for understanding and gaining attention receiving the highest share.[11]

Reason	Percentage
Encouraging thought, understanding of ideas, phenomena, procedures and values.	33%
Checking understanding, knowledge and skills.	30%
Gaining attention to task, to enable the teacher to move towards teaching point in the hope of eliciting a specific and obscure point, as a warm-up activity for pupils.	28%
Review, revision, recall, reinforcement of recently learned point, reminder of earlier procedures.	23%
Management, settling down, to stop calling out by pupils, to direct attention to teacher or text, to warn them of precautions.	20%

10 G. A. Brown and R. Edmondson, Asking Questions. In E. C. Wragg (ed.), *Classroom Teaching Skills* (London: Routledge, 1989), pp. 97–120.
11 Wragg and Brown, *Questioning in the Secondary School*, p. 8.

Reason	Percentage
Specifically to teach whole class through pupil answers.	10%
To give everyone a chance to answer.	10%
Ask bright pupils to encourage others.	4%
To draw in shyer pupils.	4%
Probe children's knowledge after critical answers, redirect question to pupils who asked or to other pupils.	3%
To allow expressions of feelings, views and empathy.	3%

Activity

Working with a colleague, reread the responses from the teachers in the table above on the reasons why they asked pupils questions and rank them in order of how you use them in your classroom. Try to think of examples of questions you have asked with the intention of eliciting one of these reasons. For example, for 'review, revision and recall': 'Based on what we studied last lesson, what coastline do headlands and bays form on?'

All of these aims are key to promoting a learning culture within your classroom. Alongside these intentions, Morgan and Saxton suggest that questions have five core purposes:

1. The process of asking pupils questions means teachers can ensure they are involved in the lesson.

2. When pupils answer a question, it provides them with the opportunity to share their views on the topic of discussion.

3. When teachers ask pupils a question, it allows other pupils to hear different perspectives from their peers.

4. Asking different types of questions enables teachers to control the flow of their lesson, not only with respect to learning but also to ensure that pupil behaviour is maintained.

5. Questioning pupils at different points in the lesson provides teachers with valuable information which helps to determine what they have learned and therefore what to cover in subsequent lessons.[12]

In essence, asking questions brings many benefits, and the more strategic we are as classroom practitioners with our use of questions, the more likely we are to support our pupils to learn. This was echoed by Rosenshine in his ten principles of instruction, one of which was dedicated to asking questions: 'Questions allow a teacher to determine how well the material has been learned and whether there is a need for additional instruction. The most successful teachers ask a large number of questions.'[13] While Rosenshine indicated that the best teachers ask lots of questions, as we have seen, not all questions equate to supporting learning. We will explore this later on when we consider what it means to ask the right questions.

....

12 N. Morgan and J. Saxton, *Teaching, Questioning and Learning* (London: Routledge, 1991).

13 B. Rosenshine, Principles of Instruction: Research-Based Strategies That All Teachers Should Know, *American Educator* (spring 2012), 12–19 at 14. Available at: https://www.aft.org/sites/default/files/Rosenshine.pdf.

Rosenshine is not the only researcher who has championed the power of questions; others have also emphasised the importance of using questions in the classroom to promote learning. In 1978, Gall et al. conducted a two-week experiment with a group of elementary school classes based on the topic of ecology. The study involved one group of classes reading a textbook each day and then answering questions set by the teacher, while the other classes read the same textbook but didn't engage in answering questions from the teacher. At the end of the study, the group who participated in the question session from the teacher performed better than the control group.[14]

> **Pedagogy reflection:** When teachers ask the right questions and involve pupils, there is a greater probability that it will boost pupil performance.

When I first started teaching, the thought of asking pupils questions was daunting – and when pupils asked me difficult questions I would find this equally challenging. This is because I was unsure how to respond if I didn't know the answer instantly, as I was still developing my own subject knowledge and getting my head around the curriculum. I hadn't yet developed a strong repertoire of knowledge examples and non-examples, and I was unaware of the common misconceptions that pupils might present in lessons. It was a dilemma: I didn't know all the answers but I felt that I should know them to build my credibility as a new teacher. I found it unsettling when a pupil asked a challenging question and I couldn't answer it – after all, I was their teacher.

In the first few years of my career, I would seek to move on quickly when I was asked these difficult questions and put the focus on the flow of questions going the other way – from teacher to

---

14 M. D. Gall, B. A. Ward, D. C. Berliner, L. S. Cahen, P. H. Winne, J. D. Elashoff and G. C. Stanton, Effects of Questioning Techniques and Recitation on Student Learning, *American Educational Research Journal*, 15 (1978), 175–199.

pupils – by asking another question. Inevitably, I was stifling the opportunity to use questions to stimulate thinking and promote learning. I was using it as a method to pull knowledge out and affirm what I believed the select few pupils I chose to answer a question should know. Not only was I doing all the thinking, but I was also asking lots of questions to avoid getting into a meaningful conversation about the learning for fear of revealing that I didn't know the answer. I was focused on asking low-level cognitive questions that emphasised factual recall based around knowledge with which I felt secure.

On reflection, this was one of the key issues I needed to develop. The questions I asked weren't challenging enough because they were questions I felt sufficiently confident that the pupils would be able to answer, and therefore avoid that awful silence. If I wanted to challenge pupils, I would need to get them to discover the answer from a pre-prepared worksheet or through a research task – that is, shifting the flow from teacher to pupil.

While getting pupils to ask more of their own questions is a skill we want them to develop, it isn't something we should be doing during the initial phase of instruction, when they are novices in the field in which we want them to become experts, especially if it is new information that hasn't been taught previously. Considering prior knowledge is an important component when asking powerful questions in the classroom if we are to support knowledge retention and learning over time. We will explore this more deeply as we move through the chapters.

When it comes to answering questions, as teachers we may not know the answer to every question, despite taking the time in advance to prepare our explanations and anticipating the potential questions and misconceptions our pupils may have. This is okay and not something we should feel bad about. If while reading *Powerful Questioning* you feel that you haven't got questioning right, that is to be expected. The art of questioning isn't something we master overnight; it takes time and lots of practice to get it right. Every teacher, no matter how many years of experience they may have, will be working on the execution of their questions. However, I hope that this book offers a guide that will empower you to master the use of questions in the classroom in such a way that will contribute towards supporting your learners' retention of knowledge.

> **Pedagogy reflection:** When pupils ask questions, we may not always know the answer straight away, but this should be something we embrace and look to develop over time.

So, what do we mean when we talk about asking a question? Asking questions is a natural act, and I imagine that as you sat down to read you may have asked or answered a question. But, the art of asking effective questions is not so easy. How many times have you asked a question and wondered whether you could have phrased it more clearly? There are times when we ask a question and it leads to a puzzled expression on the face of the recipient. While we may believe that our question is clear, others may perceive it differently. There will either be an awkward silence or a response such as, 'What do you mean?' 'I'm not really sure what you're asking me.' 'Please can you rephrase the question?' Consequently, you have to rephrase the original question.

Equally, there will be times when someone may answer your question based on what they believe you want to hear. This could be to enable them to get on with their day, or to not hurt your feelings, or to avoid revealing something they don't want you to know about. Therefore, the authenticity of the question–response mode will be influenced by the relationship between the questioner and questionee.

Also, we often ask people questions assuming they have some prior knowledge of the subject matter. Let's consider the following example: 'What did you think of the TV series *The Crown*?' The recipient's answer will be based on whether they have watched, read about or heard something about the series. Their response will be determined by this prior knowledge, a schema that has been developed or not. In the classroom, this prior knowledge will influence the level of participation and the degree to which pupils can access the question. We will explore this later on in Chapter 3 when we unpick the role of questioning in checking for understanding.

There are many variables involved in the process of devising, asking, interpreting and answering a question. When we consider the complex web of interactions involved, we can begin to appreciate why questions can have both a positive and negative influence on learning. With this in mind, taking time to carefully plan our use of questions in the classroom can go a long way towards making them a tool to support learning. We will look at strategies that you could use when preparing your own questions in the final chapter.

Some of the early research into questioning in the classroom indicates that it can be a powerful instructional tool to facilitate learning,[15] but it is all too easy to use questioning ineffectively. Some of the common errors include:

- A large proportion of questions flowing in one direction only to control the classroom rather than encourage pupils to think.

- Teachers answering their own questions before giving pupils time to respond.

- Asking too many rhetorical questions.

- Asking leading questions.

- Teachers spending a greater proportion of their time asking lower level cognitive questions.

- Accepting wrong answers without correcting them.

- Asking challenging questions at the beginning of learning new knowledge when the foundations of understanding are insecure.

....

15 Wragg and Brown, *Questioning in the Secondary School*, p. 11.

- Not encouraging pupils to develop their answer after an initial response.

- Accepting non-explanatory responses.

- Asking irrelevant questions not linked to the learning sequence to fill a void in the lesson.

- Asking too many questions at once, overwhelming pupils' working memory and causing cognitive overload.

- Calling on a selected few pupils every lesson who are keen to answer questions.

- Not allowing pupils time to think between asking and answering the question.

- Focusing on what pupils already know, thereby generating a false picture of understanding.

Activity

Reflect on the list of common errors above and consider those you have experienced with questioning. For example, let's take the fifth bullet point: *Teachers spending a greater proportion of their time asking lower level cognitive questions.* Write down the questions you asked your pupils in the last lesson. How many of them were low-level cognitive questions?

So, what can we do to avoid these common errors? This is the aim of *Powerful Questioning*: I will explore – through analysing the research, speaking with practising teachers and drawing on my own experience – a range of strategies to implement in the classroom to enhance the use of questioning as a pedagogical tool.

In the first chapter, we will consider why we ask questions, reflecting on the theories around the evolution of asking questions from early childhood and how it can support cognitive development, as well as considering what the hallmarks of a good question look like. The chapter spotlight shines on Bradley Busch, a psychologist who works in education, who shares his views on the psychology of using questions and reflects on their role in the classroom.

In Chapter 2, the focus shifts to looking at the foundations to building a questioning culture in the classroom, exploring the different factors that can contribute to this as well as strategies to support its implementation. In the first part of this chapter, we will reflect on the reasons why pupils' participation in answering questions varies and assess a range of strategies to increase it for all children. At the end of the chapter, Catherine Owen, an experienced middle leader and geography teacher, outlines how she promotes participation in her classroom.

Chapter 3 investigates the use of questioning to check for understanding, exploring how teachers can use questions to move from lower order to higher order cognitive questions to assess learning. When using questions, teachers often focus heavily on asking low-level cognitive questions (which get pupils to recall isolated knowledge with minimal thought or application) and managerial questions (to organise day-to-day classroom procedures). This doesn't mean that we shouldn't be asking these types of questions to check for understanding or to build routines, but we will find out how a variety of lower order to higher order cognitive questions is important to support learning. Stuart Pryke shines a light on how he uses questioning as a responsive teaching tool.

In Chapter 4, we consider how questioning can be used to diagnose learning, develop pupils' metacognition and promote self-regulation. Pupils knowing and understanding what they have learned is an important part of the learning process. Alongside this, we will discover how questions can be used to support the mentoring of teachers. Mentoring in schools aims to build relationships between colleagues to provide a springboard for professional development. Haili Hughes joins us to share how funnel questioning can empower teachers.

In the final chapter, I will summarise the key takeaways from the book by outlining five core principles for powerful questioning in the classroom: sequencing, presenting and framing, pausing, gathering and processing, and redirecting. This chapter will bring together the key discussions from each of the chapters to provide a series of recommendations for using powerful questions based on the research and practical experiences.

Let's begin by considering why we ask questions.

Chapter 1

Why do we ask questions?

Teachers are so used to asking questions that they fail to analyse why or how they do it.

Patricia Blosser[1]

In this chapter, we will:

- Reflect on where the idea of a question began and a working definition for the classroom.
- Explore the theories behind asking questions.
- Reflect on the purpose of asking questions.
- Consider how questioning supports cognitive development.
- Review different types of questions.
- Consider the cognitive demands associated with asking questions.
- Look at the hallmarks of a good question.

1   P. E. Blosser, *How to … Ask the Right Questions* (Washington, DC: National Science Teachers Association, 1991), p. 2.

17

Where does it all begin?

When considering the origins of the word 'question', we can find examples dating back to the Middle Ages. During the thirteenth century, the word *questioun* was used – defined as 'a philosophical or theological problem' – and during the fourteenth century, this was revised to 'an utterance meant to elicit an answer or discussion'.[2]

This second idea, that we ask a question to elicit an answer or prompt a discussion, is something rather more recognisable to what we understand today. For the purpose of this book, we will work with Cotton's suggested definition for the use of questions when working with pupils: 'In classroom settings, teacher questions are defined as instructional cues or stimuli that convey to students the content elements to be learned and directions for what they are to do and how they are to do it.'[3] Cotton believed that questions had the core purpose of encouraging pupils to be actively involved in class discussions, to develop critical thinking and to independently seek out further knowledge.

Questions are an integral part of our daily lives. We are continually considering questions to ask others or anticipating having to answer someone else's question. Of course, the question will vary in type, complexity and intention. As the questioner, we will get either the response we were expecting or we may be left wondering. There will be times when we ask a question and a puzzled look appears on the face of the recipient. On the flip side, if we are the person answering the question, we may feel either confident or potentially anxious about how to respond. So, we may just attempt to move on quickly and avoid answering.

Asking or answering questions is something we do naturally as humans, but, interestingly, as we reach adulthood there is a

....

2   See https://www.etymonline.com/word/question.
3   K. Cotton, *Classroom Questioning* (School Improvement Research Series) (Portland, OR: North West Regional Educational Laboratory, 2001), p. 1. Available at: https://educationnorthwest.org/sites/default/files/ClassroomQuestioning.pdf.

tendency to ask fewer questions. Research suggests that children's curiosity to ask questions declines when they start school, with question asking dwindling from one every two minutes to one every two hours.[4] So, why do we tend to ask fewer questions as we grow up? Let's go back to early childhood and explore where our question-asking journey begins.

From around 4 years of age, children's curiosity about the world increases and they ask their parents a lot of questions. Right from the moment they wake up to the time when they rest their tired heads, asking questions becomes almost a hobby. Parents are inundated with question after question from their child throughout the day as they look for answers about the world around them. Child psychologist Sam Wass states that children can ask up to as many as seventy-three questions a day.[5] Meanwhile, Berger cites a research study which suggests that 4-year-old British girls ask 390 questions per day.[6] Asking questions becomes second nature as children start to grow up. As a parent this can be tiring, but this is a good thing and something we shouldn't discourage. The more questions children ask, the more they develop a deeper understanding of the world around them.

Early research suggested that children ask questions to prolong a conversation rather than because they want an explanation. The reasoning was that children don't understand causality until the age of between 5 and 8. As research into the development of young children's minds has grown, there is now an increasing

---

4   S. Engel, Many Kids Ask Fewer Questions When They Start School. Here's How We Can Foster Their Curiosity, *Time* (23 February 2021). Available at: https://time.com/5941608/schools-questions-fostering-curiousity.

5   E. Elsworthy, Curious Children Ask 73 Questions Each Day – Many of Which Parents Can't Answer, Says Study, *The Independent* (3 December 2017). Available at: https://www.independent.co.uk/news/uk/home-news/curious-children-questions-parenting-mum-dad-google-answers-inquisitive-argos-toddlers-chad-valley-tots-town-a8089821.html.

6   W. Berger, *A More Beautiful Question: The Power of Inquiry* (New York: Bloomsbury, 2014), p. 4.

acceptance that children younger than the age of 5 may be able to make causal inferences about their environment.[7]

In a series of studies, Frazier and colleagues found that when adults set up strong learning environments, it can contribute towards richer conversations with children from the age of 2 years.[8] When the researchers set out to investigate the role of adults and learning environments, their initial hypothesis was to prove that the more children sought an explanation through asking questions, the more likely they would react to the adults' responses. If children were asking questions just to spark or prolong a conversation, then any answer from the adult would be enough to satisfy them. However, if in fact children were asking questions because they wanted to find out more, then the nature and length of the response from the adult would affect how they reacted.

In the first of their experiments, they examined the transcripts of conversations between six children, aged between 2 and 5 years, and their parents, siblings or other adults to investigate how they reacted to satisfactory or unsatisfactory responses to their 'how' and 'why' questions. The results indicated that even the 2-year-olds acted differently depending on the response they received. For example, if children receive some form of explanatory response, rather than a reply of 'I don't know', they are more likely to engage and ask further questions.

Even as adults, when we ask a question and receive a non-explanatory response like, 'I'm not sure' or 'You'll need to ask someone else', the engagement in follow-up questions is somewhat limited. It is a conversation killer.

7   M. Severns, Why Ask Why? New Research Looks at Children's Questions, *New America* (30 November 2009). Available at: https://www.newamerica. org/education-policy/early-elementary-education-policy/early-ed-watch/ why-ask-why-new-research-looks-at-childrens-questions.
8   B. N. Frazier, S. A. Gelman and H. M. Wellman, Young Children Prefer and Remember Satisfying Explanations, *Journal of Cognition and Development*, 17(5) (2016), 718–736. https://doi.org/10.1080/15248372.2015.1098649

Activity

Take a moment to consider a time when you have asked a question and the person you are asking replies with a non-explanatory response. A mixture of emotions may follow, including a lack of confidence in the person to whom you have asked the question, which may lead to a reluctance to ask them any further questions.

Consider the following scenario: you are looking to purchase a new mobile phone but you aren't sure which contract would be most beneficial for your needs. When speaking to the store representative, you receive a series of non-explanatory responses like, 'I don't know' and 'I'm not sure', leaving you in the same situation as when you arrived at the shop. Inevitably, you won't have confidence in the representative and will leave in search of another retailer who will be able to answer your questions and support you in purchasing a suitable mobile phone contract. Non-explanatory responses can result in people being less likely to engage in further conversation and asking fewer questions.

Pedagogy reflection: In the classroom, we want our pupils to be inquisitive – asking lots of questions to prompt them to think about what they are learning.

The more curious a child becomes, the more questions they will ask. Questions play an important role in cognitive development, as outlined in a research study by Chouinard: 'Children are skilled at recruiting needed information from the very start of their ability to communicate with parents; the primary purpose of their question-asking behaviors is to gather information, and they are skilled at generating efficient questions that allow them to solve the problems that face them.'[9] Therefore, asking lots of questions allows children to build their schemas. They can provide the missing piece to the knowledge puzzle and create a lightbulb moment. Chouinard believes the following points are key to using questions to support cognitive development:

1. Children must ask questions that harvest information.

2. Children need to receive 'informative answers' to their questions.

3. Children must be genuinely inspired to seek information, not simply want attention.

4. The questions must be 'relevant and of potential use to their cognitive development'.

5. There must be evidence that the questions 'achieve some change of knowledge state' in the children.[10]

> **Pedagogy reflection:** Asking lots of powerful questions helps to build mental models. How can we channel these questions to build schema and promote retention?

As a parent myself, I remember being asked lots of questions when my two children, Abigail and Harry, were growing up; some more challenging than others. This included the question 'Why?' which would follow when I wouldn't allow them to do something. It is the ultimate question and leads to the same question being repeated when the answer you give isn't satisfactory:

---

9   M. M. Chouinard, Children's Questions: A Mechanism for Cognitive Development, *Monographs of the Society for Research in Child Development*, 72(1) (2007): vii–ix, 1–112; discussion 113–126 at 108. https://doi.org/10.1111/j.1540-5834.2007. 00412.x

10 Chouinard, Children's Questions, 12.

'Why?' 'Why?' 'Why?' Some of the most challenging questions that children ask their parents are:

1. Why is the sky blue?

2. Where do babies come from?

3. Where does water come from?

4. Why do people get sick?

5. What happens when you die?

6. Where does God live?

7. Where are my socks?

8. Why?[11]

Questions are an integral part of our lives. As we grow up, we continue to ask questions to find out more about the world, to seek clarification or to ask someone to do something. We ask questions on a daily basis, each of them with a different purpose.

Activity

Think about the questions you have asked today. What was their function? Did you get the answers you wanted or expected?

In the classroom, the purpose of questions will vary, from prompting a routine ('Have you written the homework in your planner?') to prompting recall ('Who was Henry VIII?') as well as encouraging deeper thought ('Why do trees reduce flood risk?'). In the last week, how many of these three questions have you asked? What proportion have you asked in a lesson or over a series of

11   M. Lynch, 10 Common Questions Kids Ask and How You Should Answer, *The Advocate* (25 October 2018). Available at: https://www.theedadvocate.org/10-common-questions-kids-ask-answer.

lessons? A 1993 study by Wragg recorded over 1,000 questions by primary school teachers. The questions were divided into three categories: managerial, information/data and higher order. The study indicated that a larger proportion of questions were in the managerial and information/data zone, with fewer questions asked to promote deeper thinking, as shown in the table below.[12]

Type of question	Percentage
Managerial	57%
Information/data	35%
Higher order	8%

Pedagogy reflection: Managerial questions are an important component of our classrooms when we are building scholarly habits, but as a culture of learning becomes the social norm, the pendulum should swing to asking questions that initiate thought beyond recall.

Activity

Write out the questions you have asked in the last few lessons or work with a colleague and write down the different questions you both ask during a lesson. Organise your questions into the three different types – managerial, information/data and higher order. What is the most common type of question you ask in a lesson?

12 E. C. Wragg, *Primary Teaching Skills* (London: Routledge, 1993), cited in Wragg and Brown, *Questioning in the Secondary School*, p. 9.

In another study by Suydam, teachers of mathematics spent up to one-third of the lesson asking questions. However, 80% of the questions were at the lowest cognitive level – recalling knowledge and comprehension (for example, 'What is the formula to find the area of a rectangle?'). Fewer teachers asked questions at a higher cognitive level which would prompt pupils to problem-solve through deeper thinking.[13]

In many of the research studies identified so far, there is a clear pattern of teachers asking a higher proportion of lower cognitive questions compared to higher cognitive questions. In Gall's synthesis of research on teachers' questioning, the pattern of lower vs higher level questions suggested that only 20% of questions posed in classrooms require higher order thinking.[14] If this is the case, how often are pupils merely just participating in the question–response mode (i.e. the teacher asks a question and the pupil responds with minimal thought)?

A study by Wimer et al. looked at whether the type of questions asked in urban elementary classrooms differed between boys and girls. The findings indicated that girls were not questioned any differently in terms of frequency or level of demand compared with boys. However, both genders experienced being asked fewer higher order questions that prompted them to think beyond knowledge recall. Alongside this inconclusive difference between the genders, the study highlighted that boys were more likely to be called upon if they didn't volunteer an answer to a question.[15]

The research demonstrates a disproportionate use of questions in schools. In subsequent chapters, we will consider how this pattern can be changed to promote the more powerful use of questions in the classroom.

---

13 M. N. Suydam, Research Report: Questions?, *Arithmetic Teacher*, 32(6) (1985), 18.
14 M. D. Gall, Synthesis of Research on Teachers' Questioning, *Educational Leadership*, 42(3) (1984), 40–47.
15 J. W. Wimer, C. S. Ridenour, K. Thomas and A. W. Place, Higher Order Teacher Questioning of Boys and Girls in Elementary Mathematics Classrooms, *Journal of Educational Research*, 95(2) (2001), 84–92. https://doi.org/10.1080/00220670109596576

> **Pedagogy reflection:** When pupils don't volunteer answers to questions, call on both boys and girls to contribute answers.

Glišić found that children ask three different types of questions during early childhood: cognitive, social and operational questions.[16] Cognitive questions are used to satisfy children's curiosity about themselves, others or the world around them (e.g. 'Why is the sky blue?' 'Why do I have blue eyes?'). Social questions are asked to satisfy personal needs, to share disagreement, to seek attention or to get validation (e.g. 'I don't like peas. Do I have to eat them?'). Operational questions are used to ask for help or request permission (e.g. 'Can I have an ice cream?').

As children grow up, the ratio of the types of questions changes. Up to the age of 5, the number of cognitive and operational questions increase, while the number of social questions remain relatively static. As children start preschool and early years, the number of questions they ask decreases. This pattern continues as children move through education: the older they get, the fewer questions they ask. Why might this be the case? It could be argued that as we mature and build our schemas of knowledge, we don't need to ask as many questions as we did when we were discovering more about our surroundings. Therefore, our curiosity decreases.

Activity

Pause for a minute and think about your own experiences of asking and answering questions. Based on the year groups you have taught, have you noticed a difference in the number of questions pupils ask?

16   T. Č. Glišić, Why Do Children Ask Questions: New Classification of Preschool Children's Questions, *Teaching Innovations*, 30(2) (2017), 114–127. Available at: http://www.inovacijeunastavi.rs/wp-content/uploads/Inovacije2-17en/PR08.pdf.

Could there be other factors influencing the decline in the number of questions asked? Maria Birbili from the Department of Early Childhood Education at the Aristotle University of Thessaloniki has explored how teachers can get children back on track to asking productive questions in the early years of schooling: 'studies of classroom talk suggest that the frequency and the quality of children's questions drop as soon as they begin in an early childhood setting. The way educators treat children's questions influences whether children will continue to pose questions in the classroom.'[17]

> **Pedagogy reflection:** Reflecting on your own classroom practice, do you create the right conditions where pupils feel confident in asking and answering questions? For example, do you promote a culture where getting questions wrong is part of learning and nothing they should feel ashamed of?

As children grow up, the pressure of their peers and the influence this has on classroom behaviour increases. Peer relationships can be more impactful in the classroom than teacher–pupil relationships, with the associated fear of losing face in front of their friends a potentially overwhelming factor in why the number of questions asked reduces as pupils mature. We will explore this further in Chapter 2, looking in more depth at the possible reasons for variations in question contribution, considering the research and the strategies we can use to create a culture where pupils feel confident to both ask and answer questions. Essentially, as classroom practitioners, our ultimate goal is to reverse the trend indicated in the research.

....

17   M. Birbili, *Supporting Young Children to Ask Productive Questions* (Research in Practice) (Watson, ACT: Early Childhood Australia, 2017), cited in S. Briggs, The Importance of Kids Asking Questions, *informED* (25 March 2020). Available at: https://www.opencolleges.edu.au/informed/features/importance-kids-asking-questions.

The purpose and benefit of asking powerful questions

Questions are a vital tool to promote thought and encourage social interaction. Socrates believed in the power of questioning to such an extent that he argued for his students to increase their knowledge in order to engage in rich questioning and thoughtful discussions: 'I know you won't believe me, but the highest form of human excellence is to question oneself and others.'[18]

There are many reasons why we ask questions which may include: to encourage discussion, to gather information, to prompt thought, to share interests and to determine the outcome of initial thought. Some of the most successful teams in the world ask lots of questions. In 2004, a study investigating the role of communication in the performance of business teams was conducted at the Massachusetts Institute of Technology by Chilean psychologist Marcial Losada and organisational behavioural researcher Emily Heaphy. The research indicated a strong correlation between the team's curiosity and openness and the organisation's performance. From their research, Losada and Heaphy concluded there was a strong link: high-performing teams learned and collaborated to a larger extent which helped them to develop greater synergy.[19]

Vogt et al. believe that asking a powerful question brings the following benefits:

- generates curiosity in the listener

- stimulates reflective conversation

- is thought-provoking

....

18 Quoted in J. Sutton, Socratic Questioning in Psychology: Examples and Techniques, *Positive Psychology* (19 June 2020). Available at: https://positivepsychology.com/socratic-questioning.

19 M. Losada and E. Heaphy, The Role of Positivity and Connectivity in the Performance of Business Teams: A Nonlinear Dynamics Model, *American Behavioral Scientist*, 47(6) (2004), 740–765. https://doi.org/10.1177/0002764203260208

- surfaces underlying assumptions

- invites creativity and new possibilities

- generates energy and forward movement

- channels attention and focuses inquiry

- stays with participants

- touches a deep meaning

- evokes more questions[20]

Alongside these benefits, Vogt et al. suggest there are three architectural dimensions to powerful questions:

1. **Construction** – is the question aimed at generating low or higher order thinking?

2. **Scope** – to what extent does the question provide freedom for the respondent?

3. **Assumptions** – what can be inferred from the context/meaning of the question?[21]

With this in mind, by giving careful consideration to the structure of the question we can affect the cognitive demand. In any classroom, a variety of question stems will be used to frame and present a question to pupils. In many cases, these questions will be determined by the subject discipline, but Vogt et al. state that the following six core question types will be a dominant feature. Each has a different purpose.

1. When we ask a *when* question, the purpose is to seek an answer based on time or a timeline of events, either in the past or the future (e.g. 'When was the Battle of Hastings?' 'When do you think France will next win the World Cup?').

---

20 E. E. Vogt, J. Brown and D. Isaacs, *The Art of Powerful Questions: Catalyzing Insight, Innovation, and Action* (Mill Valley, CA: Whole Systems Associates, 2003), p. 4.

21 Vogt et al., *The Art of Powerful Questions*, p. 4.

2. A *where* question has the purpose of looking to establish the location of something (e.g. 'Where do you find polar bears?' 'Where is the Eiffel Tower?').

3. Asking a *who* question involves gathering information about a person, group or people or organisation responsible for causing, influencing or changing an event/situation (e.g. 'Who was responsible for the invention of the light bulb?' 'Who were responsible for the introduction of the new behaviour policy?').

4. A *how* question is seeking to find reasons or different factors that may have caused something to happen (e.g. 'How do professional athletes prepare for a tournament?' 'How does an electrical circuit work?').

5. When we ask a *what* question, we are encouraging the pupil to provide a descriptive response or to elaborate on something (e.g. 'What do bees make?' 'What makes you feel happy?').

6. When we ask a *why* question, we are looking for an explanation from the person we ask (e.g. 'Why do rivers flood?' 'Why does it rain more in Scotland?').

The typology of questions

Adjoining, elevating, clarifying and funnelling

Questions can be aimed at addressing various levels of cognition, ranging from the recall of memorised facts to processes that require deep critical thinking. Depending on the type of question we ask, this will inevitably lead to a different outcome, and possibly outcomes we may not have initially intended or expected. Consider the following four types of questions: adjoining, elevating, clarifying, and funnelling. Each one can be used to steer a conversation towards a particular goal. In any discussion, you might need to use a combination of these question types to achieve your intention.

When we use *clarifying* questions, the goal is to gain a clearer understanding of what has been said. There will be times when we are asked a question that we may not hear properly the first time because of other distractions ('Can you repeat the question?') or we need further clarification ('Could you expand on what you mean?'). Sometimes we may not feel comfortable about asking these questions because they reveal our own weaknesses. When we ask for more information, it may suggest that either we have not have been listening or that we lack knowledge and understanding around the topic of discussion. This is common in our classrooms where many pupils lack confidence in asking for clarification if they haven't understood the task set or the knowledge recall question asked. In Chapter 2, we will consider how to remove some of these barriers to encourage pupils to use clarifying questions when it is necessary.

In contrast, *adjoining* questions are used to consider other components related to the conversation or discussion. We can use (or encourage the use) of these questions to deepen our understanding of the topic we are studying. Adjoining questions are helpful when we want pupils to make links and connections between previously taught information and transfer it to new contexts – for example, 'How might this apply somewhere else?' or 'How might this affect someone else?' In the classroom, we might use adjoining questions after a series of lessons to review information in a new context or when moving from guided to independent practice. For instance, if the pupils are studying deforestation in tropical rainforests, the teacher could use adjoining questions to prompt them to relate it to the importance of forests as carbon sinks from an earlier unit on climate change.

A *funnelling* question is multifunctional. By using a series of sequenced funnelling questions, we can move from a narrow point to a more broader discussion. The route the question-asker takes will be dependent on the pupils' response to the narrower questions asked initially. Based on their responses, the questions could broaden or dive deeper by challenging any misconceptions or prompt elaboration on the initial response to understand how the answer was arrived at – for example, 'How did you do that?' or 'Why did that cause the change to happen?'

Finally, the use of *elevating* questions can assist in raising wider issues and allow pupils to see the bigger picture; it can be harder for us to gain a broad perspective when we are involved in a deep conversation. For example, when considering how to solve a problem we might ask, 'Let's take a moment to reflect – how do all the pieces of information connect?' Elevating questions can help us to develop connections between different pieces of knowledge and support problem-solving.

Open and closed

Two common question types that you might be more familiar with are open and closed questions. An open question allows someone to respond with greater freedom and detail by drawing on their prior knowledge. Examples of open questions you might ask pupils include:

- What is hydraulic action?

- What was the main cause of the First World War?

- Why do we use a semicolon?

- Why do we need to tackle climate change?

If the question can be answered from a limited set or with either a simple yes/no or true/false, then it is classed as a closed question. Examples of closed questions we might ask pupils include:

- Which of the following is the correct definition of weathering …?

- Romeo is from the house of Capulet – true or false?

- What is the next step in the process of photosynthesis?
- Which of the following is the correct use of a comma …?

Convergent and divergent

A convergent question is similar to a closed question and requires the respondent to give a predetermined answer. Examples might include:

- Thinking from the writer's perspective, what are her possible motivating reasons for writing …?
- What factors will increase the speed of the propeller?

In comparison, a divergent question allows for a wider range of possible responses, much like an open question. This type of question is powerful when you want the respondent to think creatively and build a response using their wider experiences. Examples might include:

- What are the reasons why this decision was made?
- What other factors will cause the changes to happen?

Predictive and hypothetical

Predictive questions can allow the respondent to indicate their thoughts on the topic of discussion and provide greater flexibility for them to decide on what they believe might happen. For example:

- Based on what has just happened, what do you think will happen next?
- Reflecting on your own experience, what might happen if …?
- What do you think the outcome will be when …?

In contrast, hypothetical questions are a useful tool to allow the respondent to move beyond their initial thoughts and create opportunities to anticipate what might happen. For example:

- If the erosion were to continue, what problems might it create?

- If the athlete doesn't warm up, what issues might it lead to?

- What if Tybalt hadn't challenged Romeo to a duel?

Focal and funnel

With a focal question, the respondent is expected to make a decision based on the series of options presented. An example might be:

- Which of the following is the correct definition for …?

Funnel questions can also be referred to as multiple choice questions because there are options from which to choose, and then, from the option(s) chosen, further questioning to expand on the decision made. For example:

- Which of the following is the correct definition for …?

- Why are the other options incorrect?

Organising and valuing

When we use organising and valuing questions, we are asking the respondent to order, contrast, rank, prioritise and combine. These questions could be linked with the other question types we have already discussed in this chapter. With these types of questions, people with prior knowledge of the topic may find it easier to deduce the correct answer. Some examples of how we might ask these two question types include:

- What would be the correct sequence for the formation of a wave-cut platform?

- Which of the following items of clothing belong together …?

- Which of the following factors would come first …?

- If you were to rank the following causes of flooding, which one would you place as the number one cause …?

This brief survey demonstrates the broad range of questions available, depending on what cognitive processes and demands we wish to utilise. The question types we choose will be dependent on the reason we are asking the question and what information we are looking to gather as a result. We will explore further the art of choosing the right question in Chapter 2.

The cognitive demands of a question

Based on their typology, the questions we ask can be grouped into those that generate lower order or higher order thinking. One of the most recognised taxonomies related to the progression of lower to higher order thinking is Bloom's taxonomy. It was first devised and introduced in 1956 by American educational psychologist Benjamin Bloom with the aim of categorising learning progression, moving from knowledge at the bottom of the pyramid and advancing towards evaluation (the most challenging) at the top.[22] Ever since its introduction, it has become a significant blueprint in the education world, referred to in teacher training and used by teachers when planning lessons and sequences of learning.

....

22 B. Bloom, M. Englehart, E. Furst, W. Hill and D. Krathwohl, *Taxonomy of Educational Objectives: The Classification of Educational Goals. Handbook I: Cognitive Domain* (New York and Toronto: Longmans, Green, 1956). See also M. Hall, A Guide to Bloom's Taxonomy, *The Innovative Instructor Blog* (30 January 2015). Available at: https://ii.library.jhu.edu/2015/01/30/a-guide-to-blooms-taxonomy.

In recent years, Bloom's taxonomy has come under scrutiny because some interpretations have focused on getting to the higher order skills at the top of the pyramid as quickly as possible. While the higher order skills are important, the skills at the bottom (knowledge and understanding) are to some extent even more important. In fact, we could argue that they are essential because we can't analyse, synthesise or evaluate successfully without knowing and understanding. They provide the foundation that enables us to develop higher order thinking.

We can demonstrate this through an everyday example, such as being asked to evaluate a product as a customer. Unless you have bought the product, spent time exploring its features and experienced occasions when some of those features might not have worked, you would struggle to review it because your knowledge and understanding wouldn't be secure. Your evaluation would be surface level and based on what you might have heard or read from other sources.

There are times in our classrooms where we might move too quickly from surface to deeper level questioning without checking that our pupils' knowledge is secure. I know that I have been there myself: as pupils transition to independent practice, there can be a sea of raised hands and puzzled faces as they struggle to evaluate, assess or be creative. As professional question-askers, one of our essential roles as teachers is to check that pupils have a clear understanding of the core concepts and processes in our subjects before we ask them to demonstrate higher level skills.

We can exemplify this by using the following example of a question that pupils might be asked in a geography classroom:

Evaluate the strategies used to sustainably manage urban transport.

In order for a pupil to be able to answer this question successfully, they will need to have knowledge of the following:

- The challenges facing cities.

- The concepts of global warming and climate change.

- What sustainability means.

- What strategies can be used in cities to be more sustainable.

Once pupils have this knowledge, they would then need to utilise it to understand:

- The environmental problems created by transport systems, such as the impact of air pollution on people, plants and other animals.

- How cities are contributing towards global warming and climate change.

- The impact of rising greenhouse gases on the planet.

- Why sustainability is important for people now and for future generations.

- How different strategies can contribute towards cities becoming more sustainable in the future.

Only once pupils have gained this knowledge and developed an understanding of how it fits into the context of cities can they begin to evaluate the costs and benefits of using the different strategies. This example illustrates how the role of knowledge and understanding are the foundation that can enable pupils to apply the more complex skills higher up in Bloom's taxonomy. The questions leading up to pupils attempting the higher order skills will be key in ensuring they know and understand the different aspects of managing urban transport. The initial questions that build up to the application task could be used to recall knowledge and promote retrieval practice.

Therefore, while higher order questions can activate deeper thinking, lower order questions that aim to check knowledge and understanding are essential:

> Higher-order questions elicit deeper and critical thinking … This does not mean that lower-order questions should not be asked. It is appropriate to ask questions to address all cognitive domains as long as the desired learning outcome is kept in mind and a good mix of questions is used during each teaching session.[23]

Activity

Think of a typical higher order question you might ask your pupils. Annotate the question to consider the knowledge and understanding they would need to know in order to answer it successfully. How might you change your approach based on this insight? What type of questions could you ask as you build up to the pupils answering this main question? Make a note of these as well.

Whether we are using questions to encourage pupils to recall facts and figures or to provide a more extended response that digs deeper to promote critical thinking, we should consider using a range of question types moving from lower order to higher order chained questions in a sequence. This will form one of the key principles to using powerful questions in the classroom – the concept of sequencing – which we will explore further in Chapter 5.

23 T. Tofade, J. Elsner and S. T. Haines, Best Practice Strategies for Effective Use of Questions as a Teaching Tool, *American Journal of Pharmaceutical Education*, 77(7), article 155. Available at: https://www.ncbi.nlm.nih.gov/pmc/articles/PMC3776909.

The hallmarks of a good question

So far, we have established that asking and answering questions is a typical feature of the classroom whether it is teacher to pupil, pupil to teacher or pupil to pupil. Alongside this, we know that there are a range of question types at our disposal with each one looking to elicit different information, whether that is to recall facts or demonstrate a higher degree of understanding through prompting deeper thinking by encouraging pupils to evaluate or assess.

But the power of a question lies in its quality, not the quantity. We can ask lots of questions but they may not have the impact we expect. In fact, they might have a negative impact on learning if we only seek to clarify what pupils know (i.e. not prompting beyond surface-level thinking) or, as we have seen earlier in this chapter, asking questions without establishing prior knowledge beforehand. However, if we know the characteristics of a good question, then we can plan to maximise their potential to impact positively on learning.

Barell suggested what the hallmarks of a good question consist of:

- A good question reflects a genuine desire to find a deep feeling for wanting to know more than we already know.

- A good question helps us to think – it is one that is transcendent, one that helps us move beyond the immediate data or experience.[24]

Barell's suggestions link to what we have discussed so far in this chapter: that questions should stimulate thought and a desire to want to find out more. Engendering this curiosity in our classrooms through the questions we ask will contribute towards generating a desire to want to find out more.

---

24 J. Barell, *Developing More Curious Minds* (Alexandria, VA: Association for Supervision and Curriculum Development, 2003).

Let's consider a typical scenario in an English classroom. A teacher asks the following question:

Who was Bob Cratchit?

If pupils already know who Bob Cratchit is from their previous studies, this wouldn't generate a desire to want to find out more because they already know who Bob Cratchit is. This is where knowing your pupils' prior knowledge is key when devising and framing questions. Consider the alternative question below based on the same topic:

How does Bob Cratchit illustrate the challenges faced by people experiencing poverty during the Victorian era?

A change to the question asked allows for a deeper level of thinking, helping the pupils, as Barell suggested, to 'move beyond the immediate data or experience'. Of course, how you ask this question (in comparison to the first one) will depend on the pupils' prior knowledge and what you know about the teaching group. This is where using questioning as a tool to check for understanding plays an important part in improving learning and retention in the classroom. We will explore this further in Chapter 3.

Barell's second point indicates the importance of the key principles I will outline in Chapter 5 around sequencing our questions to move from surface to deeper level thinking, which encourages pupils to use their knowledge and understanding. In the example from *A Christmas Carol*, a sequence of questions might begin with a recall on who Bob Cratchit is to bring the information back into working memory and then to build on this with the follow-up question, which promotes intentional thinking beyond what the pupils can recall.

For example, instead of asking, 'Who was Bob Cratchit?' the teacher might ask, 'What do we know about Bob Cratchit?'

Alongside the characteristics outlined by Barell, Dantonio highlights four approaches that teachers can employ to develop and deliver effective questions. They should:

1. Contain words that are easily understood by pupils.

2. Be stated simply, without being cluttered with additional questions or explanations.

3. Focus the pupil on the content being asked.

4. Identify the individual thinking operation pupils should use in answering the question.[25]

The final point on the 'individual thinking operation' is an important one to consider when planning what questions to ask. This builds on what we discussed earlier on in this chapter when we considered the different types of questions at teachers' disposal. Based on this research, here is a potential list of characteristics to consider when designing questions:

- Use words that are familiar to pupils.

- Use one thinking operation at a time (e.g. avoid double commands in one question such as 'how' and 'why').

- Aim to prompt thinking, with the answer not always immediately obvious.

- Provide some guidance so the answer isn't completely illusive.

Both Barell and Dantonio provide some considerations for creating good questions in our classrooms, and their suggestions indicate that taking time to plan the questions we are going to ask is an important component in getting questioning right. With

---

25 M. Dantonio, *How Can We Create Thinkers? Questioning Strategies That Work for Teachers* (Bloomington, IN: National Education Service, 1990).

this in mind, consider the following steps when thinking about the questions you want to ask pupils in your lesson:

- Spend time in department meetings looking at specific learning intentions in your subject and consider what questions you could ask. Several carefully planned questions based on the content being studied is far more beneficial compared with lots of unplanned questions.

- When asking challenging questions that promote deliberate hard thinking, dissect the key words used in your question to check that pupils understand them. A question is only powerful if your pupils understand what you are asking them, and building this into your lesson can support pupils in the thinking process. For example, what it means to evaluate or assess in history can be very different to geography. Do your pupils understand the difference?

- Ask one question at a time. Avoid overburdening pupils' working memory by asking multiple questions that require different thinking operations.

- Ask questions related to what the pupils have been learning, and consider their prior knowledge before presenting a series of questions.

Activity

Spend some time thinking about the questions you are going to ask in an imminent lesson. Write out the questions and refer back to the four points above. Practise asking these questions with colleagues to test whether they function as you intended.

In the case study that follows, psychologist Bradley Busch considers the psychology of asking questions.

Case study: The psychology of a question

Bradley Busch

Psychologically speaking, questions are incredibly unique in how they can help learning. I now view this as fundamental to my practice. This is because questions serve multiple purposes: they can capture attention, increase curiosity and significantly accelerate learning. And yet I always felt in the earlier parts of my career that I did not spend enough time being taught about how to use them most effectively.

Sometimes it seems that factual questions are seen as inferior compared to higher order questions, which include evaluative and divergent questions. But I don't believe a clear hierarchy exists. It shouldn't be seen as one being better than the others. This is because the quality of answers to evaluative or divergent questions significantly improves if there is a higher base level of understanding, which typically comes from factual questions.

Although it is probably true that these higher order questions do lend themselves more to developing pupils' metacognitive knowledge, there is an important trade-off to be aware of. When we ask factual questions, we typically have more control over the course of the lesson, as it is easier to predict where the conversation will flow. And when we concede control, we often concede time as well. This can be problematic when there is a lot of information to get through in a short space of time.

So, overall, I now do not see one type of question as being better than the others. I see them as complementary. I also appreciate that the context of the situation (i.e. how much my pupils already know, how much content I need to cover, how much time/control I want to give over) plays a part in deciding what type of question to ask and when. It really is a case of identifying what is the right fit for the right moment. Being able to distinguish this is probably where the science of learning meets the art of teaching.

The other challenging issue about questions is how we go about getting an answer. The two main strategies I try to maximise are cold calling and wait times. Initially, I was reluctant to cold call my pupils, due to my own worries that it would make them feel uncomfortable or picked on. However, research (and anecdotal experience) has demonstrated that after a short period of time, pupils often feel more comfortable participating when there is a culture and expectation of having to take part. Moreover, the quantity and quality of their answers improves too.

In terms of wait times, I always felt that I rushed how long I would wait for an answer after asking a question. This probably came from a misconception of what learning looks like; it is easy to think it looks like lots of engaging and snappy interactions, as opposed to the reality which can be punctuated by awkward silences. The other concern I had about how long to wait was a fear that my most able pupils would be bored while we waited for everyone else. However, research has shown that just by expanding our wait times for an additional second or two makes a significant difference to many pupils, with that extra time not demotivating the fastest pupils.[26] In doing so, it allows us to extend our reach of how many pupils we can get thinking hard and engaging in retrieval practice after we ask our questions.

....

26   M. B. Rowe, Wait Time: Slowing Down May Be a Way of Speeding Up!, *Journal of Teacher Education*, 37(1) (1986), 43–50. https://doi. org/10.1177/002248718603700110

Chapter summary and reflections

- From an early age, children's curiosity about the world increases and they begin to ask their parents lots of questions.

- Asking lots of questions allows children to build their complex network of knowledge schemas, but as they grow up the degree of open-ended questions they ask diminishes. What can you do as a classroom practitioner to reverse this trend?

- When adults create strong learning environments, it can lead to rich conversations with children as young as 2 years old. How can this be built into our approach to pupils when they begin their school journey right from reception through to post-16?

- When children receive some form of explanatory response, rather than a reply of 'I don't know', this drives further engagement and they are more likely to ask further questions. How can we foster this in our classrooms by discouraging non-explanatory responses in a positive manner?

- Questions are a vital tool in promoting thought and encouraging social interaction, but there can be times when we focus on quantity over quality. Taking time to think about the questions we ask, and why we are asking them at a particular point in our lessons, is fundamental to them being a powerful pedagogy tool that enhances learning and retention over time.

- Questions can be aimed at various levels of cognition, ranging from recall of memorised facts to processes that require deep critical thinking. How can we get this balance right in our classrooms?

- Asking a lot of questions is easy, but they may not be the right questions and result in minimal impact on learning. Planning the questions you intend to ask is an important part of the learning process. How often do you plan the questions you are going to ask pupils in your lessons?

Now that we have explored the art of asking questions, in Chapter 2 we will turn our attention to the foundations for establishing the most effective conditions for asking powerful questions in the classroom. Without this, no matter how good our questions are, their impact will be hindered.

Chapter 2

How do we foster a
questioning culture?

The act of asking questions and the consequent search for answers is key to active learning.

Christine Chin[1]

In this chapter, we will:

- Look at how culture influences classroom talk.
- Reflect on the reasons why pupils shy away from classroom talk.
- Explore the role of peer relationships in asking/responding to questions.
- Consider strategies to promote question participation and active classroom talk.
- Reflect on what powerful questioning looks like in the classroom.

Questioning in the classroom is easy, right? We ask a question, pupils respond, we ask more questions and so on. In fact,

1   C. Chin, Student-Generated Questions: Encouraging Inquisitive Minds in Learning Science, *Teaching and Learning*, 23(1), 59–67 at 59. Available at: https://repository. nie.edu.sg/bitstream/10497/292/1/TL-23-1-59.pdf.

developing a culture where pupils want to answer and ask questions is fundamentally difficult. We will explore the reasons why in this chapter.

We saw in Chapter 1 how as children grow up, the proportion of questions they ask diminishes from the more inquisitive 'why' to 'what' questions. As classroom practitioners, we want to hinder this shift. By rehearsing routines and nudging norms in our classrooms, we have the potential to engage and encourage our pupils towards greater and more meaningful participation, leading to a higher ratio of classroom talk over time. We can flip the narrative. Questions can be the vehicle for thought, but the conditions that lead to them being asked determines who comes along on the journey. If we want pupils to accompany us on this questioning voyage, we need to create and foster the right conditions for them to want to do so.

Before we begin thinking about how we can do this, let's consider the following scenarios:

It is Friday, period 5, and Tom, an early career teacher, is about to finish his first week as a full-time teacher. The final lesson of the week is with Year 9. The last lesson didn't go as well as he had expected. During his training, he was taught to plan what questions he intended to ask pupils, so he had spent some time on this. He felt prepared. When it came to asking the questions, though, the challenge was in getting pupils to respond. Too many children either didn't want to answer or just said 'I don't know'. Tom is finding his pupils' lack of participation difficult, and he is concerned that he will have similar issues in this next lesson.

Joe is a Year 8 pupil in Tom's English lesson. He enjoys the subject, and wants to be seen as hard-working by his teacher and receive praise when he gets the answers correct. The rest of his peers don't really contribute much in lessons, so he stands out as being super-keen. This means he doesn't always feel comfortable asking or answering questions for fear of being teased. So, he chooses not to participate in asking or answering as many questions as he would like. It is only in his English lessons where he feels like this.

In the early stages of my own career, I too came across difficulties similar to Tom's in my own classroom. I would ask the pupils lots of questions, firing them around the room. I was guilty of not giving them enough time to answer because I was too eager to move on or I wanted to fill the awkward silence. I thought that if I kept on asking lots of different questions, the pupils would respond automatically. For me, the challenge was knowing what to do when they didn't want to contribute. I can recall those uncomfortable moments when I was being observed and my use of questioning just didn't work. I wanted to get the lesson out of the way because I knew what the observer was going to say: participation in the classroom was intermittent and inconsistent; a few pupils were answering and dominating class discussions. I was asking questions but not everyone was coming on the learning journey with me. I knew that I needed to get more of my pupils involved in asking and answering questions, but I didn't know how.

All too often, some pupils didn't want to contribute to the discussion, and the default response was a non-explanatory 'I don't know'. At this point, I was guilty of moving swiftly on to the next pupil, often a child I knew would give me a response. Why did I do this? Because it was easier than sticking with the pupil who said they didn't know as I was never too sure how they would react if I continued to encourage them to provide an explanatory response.

> **Pedagogy reflection:** How many times have you accepted a non-explanatory response because it was more of a hassle to challenge the pupil?

One of the main reasons why I fell into the trap of accepting non-explanatory responses was because I didn't want the fall-out from insisting on meaningful participation. In a few schools where I worked, if I persisted it would inevitably lead to a negative response: 'Sir, I said I don't know, stop asking me!' or 'You can give me more time to think but I don't know.' These difficult exchanges happened because a culture of questioning was not embedded. Inevitably, I moved on from encouraging pupils to contribute because I didn't want to unsettle the dynamics of my lesson.

On reflection, moving on didn't get to the root of the reasons why my pupils didn't want to participate. I made the wrong decision and sent the subliminal message that this was acceptable. Accepting non-explanatory responses merely provided the pupils with a route out of taking part. Of course, it was the early stages of my career, so I put this down to a lack of experience – not having the confidence and underestimating the different factors that would affect pupils' willingness to contribute.

In contrast, there will be times when you get that one class where everyone wants to speak. The room is full of lots of confident individuals who all want their opinions heard. However, this enthusiasm can lead to many unheard voices. Managing this classroom climate is equally as difficult as when pupils are reluctant to join in. Finding the right balance between giving pupils the opportunity to speak and chaos erupting as they talk over the top of each other and drown out those pupils not participating is challenging. This is something teachers are not always taught to manage during their training years.

> **Pedagogy reflection:** When pupils respond with a non-explanatory response, encourage them to participate with a meaningful response.

Fast forward to today, and how I question pupils looks very different. This isn't something that happened overnight. I needed to know what factors were affecting pupil participation, so I could employ strategies to build a learning environment that would encourage better engagement. I have spent time creating an inclusive learning environment where I encourage pupils to take part and give a full response. If a pupil gives a non-explanatory response, I will either follow up with a scaffolded question to prompt a response or I will ask another pupil the question before returning to the first pupil to expand on their peer's answer. I want every pupil to feel involved and believe their contribution is valuable to the class discussion. Even if they get the answer wrong, I want them to know that this is all part of the learning process, which in my opinion is a crucial cog in building participation in the classroom.

Orlich et al. advocate the technique of positive prompting when teachers are faced with pupils who can't or don't want to provide an answer. They suggest that teachers do the following four things:

1. Clarify the question.
2. Elicit a fuller response.
3. Provide positive reinforcement to complete an incomplete response.
4. Provide positive reinforcement and redirection for an incorrect response.[2]

For this reason, I explain to pupils why asking and answering questions can support them and how making mistakes is all part

---

2   D. C. Orlich, R. J. Harder, R. C. Callahan, M. S. Trevisan and A. H. Brown, *Teaching Strategies: A Guide to Effective Instruction* (Boston, MA: Wadsworth Cengage Learning, 2010), p. 407.

of the learning process. An example of how this might look in the classroom is demonstrated below:

What is attrition … Ryan?

I don't know.

Think back to last lesson when we talked about what would be happening in seawater as the waves move. I'll come back to you in a minute. I want you to have a go at recalling what we learned because I know you can do it.

While Ryan is thinking, what is hydraulic action … Lucy?

Hydraulic action is the sheer force of the water wearing away the land.

Yes, that's correct, Lucy. Well done.

I'm coming back to you now … Ryan? Can you tell me what attrition is?

This short dialogue demonstrates how I encourage pupils not to opt out and give them further thinking time to try and come up with an answer. The most important part of this exchange is to ensure I go back to Ryan. If I don't return to him when I said I would, Ryan might believe that he can get out of contributing. As a result, I might lose credibility with him and the rest of the class for not following through on what I said.

Establishing credibility is important for future lessons. Pupils must know what your expectations are when it comes to contributing to class discussions and that they can't be a passenger in the lesson. Of course, this needs to be done in a positive way, so pupils feel they are being encouraged to participate in classroom talk rather than sanctioned for not doing so.

> **Pedagogy reflection:** Spend time building your pupils' confidence so they believe their contribution is valued.

The dynamics of classrooms means that all too often we can forget to return to pupils like Ryan, sending the message that it is okay to give a non-explanatory response. Equally, if when I return to Ryan and he still doesn't know the answer, I would need to use a different question to see if I can jog his memory about the process of attrition. This strategy of promoting participation for all pupils is just one example of how we can foster a questioning culture in our classrooms.

An alternative strategy is to change the question, so it isn't as high stakes as when first presented. When looking to determine what pupils know, asking a high-stakes question has the potential to result in some pupils automatically turning to a non-explanatory response. The following example from Rosemin, a science teacher, demonstrates how we might lower the risk and create a question that is more inviting for pupils to give it a go:

Initial high-stakes question: Why do we dream?

Revised lower stakes question: Why do you think we dream?

The amended question gives pupils an opportunity to share what they think, even if they might be unsure, because 'you think' invites an answer that doesn't necessarily need to be correct first time. This example is exemplified by Alfke and her work on unproductive and productive questions. Alfke believed that 'why' questions could be altered in the science classroom to 'what if' questions to make them more accessible, and therefore more productive, for pupils.[3]

But, what happens when a pupil gives the wrong answer to a question? I have definitely been there before, and in the past I would revert to responding with, 'That's not quite right ...' 'You're sort of there ...' 'You're kind of correct ...' or 'Yes, you're on the right lines ...' These responses are definitely aimed at encouraging future participation, but do they send the wrong message to

3   D. Alfke, Asking Operational Questions: A Basic Skill for Science Inquiry, *Science and Children*, 11(17) (1974), 18–19.

pupils? All of these examples acknowledge the pupil's response, but they could be interpreted in several ways. Without more context, 'That's not quite right' might leave the pupil wondering which part was not quite right. This might embed a misconception if it isn't addressed at this point of the discussion. Equally, 'You're kind of correct …' needs further clarification on which part was correct and why it wasn't the complete answer you were expecting.

When pupils offer an incorrect answer, the first step is to acknowledge the response in a positive way, to avoid reducing participation with other questions later on in the same lesson or subsequent lessons. Orlich suggests that teachers should avoid negative reinforcers such as 'No' or 'You are way off with that one' if you want pupils to have confidence in sharing answers.[4] But, at the same time, you don't want to provide positive reinforcement by suggesting their answer was correct if it wasn't. There is a fine balance to getting this aspect of questioning right. Think back to the four points Orlich suggested on page 53 and focus on two of them: *clarify the question* and *provide positive reinforcement and redirection to an incorrect response.*

Let's take the following scenario. Omar asks one of his Year 10 pupils a question and he gets it wrong:

What is saltation … Calvin?

It's the movement of particles by them rolling along the riverbed.

You're right that saltation is a transportation process but the particles don't roll along the riverbed. What else can you remember about how bed load moves in the river channel?

In this example, Omar provides positive reinforcement, 'You're right that saltation is …' and clarifies which part of the answer contained the error/misconception. Omar then asks an alternative

4   Orlich et al., *Teaching Strategies*, p. 407.

question to check for understanding, 'What else can you remember ...', which prompts Calvin to recall other knowledge about transportation processes. The follow-up to this conversation could be for Omar to open up the discussion as a think, pair, share activity or to ask another pupil about the process of saltation. (We explore the strategy of think, pair, share in Chapter 3.) Omar could then return to Calvin to repeat the answer. Alternatively, the framing and presenting of the alternative question could be delivered in such a way that the stakes are reduced. The newly presented question could start with, 'What do you think ...?' which reduces the pressure because Calvin is being asked to share what he thinks the answer might be.

Depending on the response, Omar might want to probe further if Calvin or another pupil in the class provides a partial answer. If a pupil offers an incomplete response, he could follow up with one of the following three questions: 'How did you arrive at that answer?', 'Can you provide an example?' or 'Can you expand on what you just said?'

'How did you arrive at that answer?' is a particularly effective follow-up question when a pupil is asked to calculate something from a data set in maths, science, geography or PE. If they arrive at the wrong answer, this supplementary question provides the teacher with the opportunity to uncover the process the pupil used to work out their answer. In some cases, this might be a common error and will give Omar the chance to explain this to the rest of the group.

Asking one of these three questions will allow you to gather more information and understand the reason for the pupil's response before deciding on what to do next. In the following classroom snapshot, David Goodwin, an assistant principal and geography teacher, provides a peek into his classroom and how he works with his pupils when faced with the wrong answers.

Classroom snapshot

David Goodwin

Every teacher experiences the awkwardness of a pupil claiming not to know an answer to a question. When this happens, the teacher might feel like she is doing a lousy job and rush to get the correct answer from someone who likely does know. However, you can follow these steps so that 'I don't know' doesn't end the discussion.

Start by asking the pupil to repeat the question back to you. Doing so will reveal whether they don't know or if they weren't listening to you. If the pupil still can't answer the question, you could direct the class to discuss their thinking with a quick think, pair, share. Then go back to the original pupil to see if they can answer the question; if they can't, select another pupil. If you get a correct answer, go back to the original pupil and ask them to repeat, rephrase or re-explain what they have just heard. If multiple pupils don't know the answer, it is clear you need to reteach the content.

Activity

Think of an example where you have had a pupil who responded with 'I don't know' to your question. What did you do next? How did you try and get that pupil to be involved and provide a response?

Before we look at further strategies to build participation, let's consider some of the possible barriers.

Barriers to classroom participation

When I was at school, I only answered a question when I was confident that I knew the right answer. This was because I didn't want to be perceived as stupid by my peers. It was all about my confidence and not wanting to feel embarrassed. On the whole, I was a conscientious pupil who wanted to achieve the best possible grades, so I would listen and write lots of notes. Even if I knew the answer, I would go red as soon as the spotlight was on me. It took me many years to control my fear of public speaking. Even when I started teaching, standing up in front of pupils, asking and answering questions was challenging.

The real challenge came when I didn't know the answer and hadn't put my hand up, but the teacher called on me anyway. The relationship I had with individual teachers had a significant influence on my willingness to contribute at this moment. Having experienced this situation as a pupil has made me very aware that I am probably teaching pupils who felt just like I did.

Take a moment to think about your own classroom experience. What kind of pupil were you? Did you actively engage in asking and answering questions? Or were you that pupil who found every way possible to remain hidden in the lesson? I asked a group of teachers about their own experience of being questioned in the classroom. Here are some of their responses:

The more comfortable I was with the other pupils in the class, the more likely I was to speak.

It depended on which class I was in … I was painfully shy and anxious that I would get the answers wrong. If I was uncomfortable, I would stare at the desk until the teacher moved on. Teachers I had good relationships with fared better.

I'd never answer unless I was chosen. I was petrified of getting it wrong or having attention on me. Also a fear of being bullied/called a swot!

It depended on the teacher – I would only answer a question if I knew the teacher didn't mind if I got it wrong. There were some teachers I was too scared to answer.

Our classrooms are dynamic environments with different personalities combining and competing to find their place. We often underestimate the role that peer-to-peer relationships have on pupils' willingness to engage in the lesson. Research has demonstrated that when pupils feel isolated from their peer group, overall academic performance will be lower.[5] I suspect that if you reflect on your current teaching groups, the degree of pupil participation will vary, with some groups more talkative and willing to answer and ask questions compared with other groups. This is normal. A multitude of factors will cause the degree of participation to vary throughout the academic year, but by considering the issues that influence this rate of participation, we can look to implement strategies that encourage pupils to ask and answer more questions.

In a typical classroom, there will be many reasons why pupils may not want to ask or answer a question. These might include:

- **Feeling shy.** Some pupils may feel uncomfortable asking and answering questions because they are naturally quiet and don't want to have attention drawn to them. These pupils will hide away from contributing and will just get on with the task set. Without realising it, these pupils can become lost in the lesson, receiving minimal interaction from peers and you as the teacher.

5   A. B. Olalekan, Influence of Peer Group Relationship on the Academic Performance of Students in Secondary Schools: A Case Study of Selected Secondary Schools in Atiba Local Government Area of Oyo State, *Global Journal of Human-Social Science*, 16(A4) (2016), 37–40.

Fear of failure. There will be times when pupils have a fear of getting something wrong, so to avoid this they actively choose not to ask or answer questions. The default response is likely to revert back to the non-explanatory 'I don't know'. Many of these pupils would prefer to be perceived as lazy by their peers than lacking in intelligence. They will have high expectations of themselves or experience additional pressure from home to succeed. All of this combined can become too all-consuming for them.

Peer pressure. No pupil wants to embarrass themselves in front of their friends. The influence of peers can be powerful in determining whether a child is willing to contribute in a lesson. Something may have happened outside of school or just before your lesson which will determine their degree of confidence in putting themselves out there. Unless a learning culture is embedded and the norm, the idea of being successful at school can lead to some pupils being unwilling to contribute for fear of being seen as overly keen or eager.

Already know it. Pupils may feel that contributing to a question won't enhance their own knowledge because they already know the answer. These pupils often don't feel challenged by the questions being asked. Allowing someone else to contribute diverts attention away from them and allows others to be involved. Pupils may do this consciously or unconsciously.

Limited value. There will be some lessons where pupils will actively avoid asking or answering a question because they don't enjoy or rate the subject. They don't believe the subject adds any value to their flight path, so doing the bare minimum is sufficient.

Context. There might be times when the context of a question may unsettle individual pupils because the subject brings up upsetting memories. For example, it may bring back unwanted recollections relating to their family or an event during the school day, resulting in them not wanting to take part in the discussion. Knowing this prior to the start of the lesson means that these pupils don't end up feeling put on the spot during a question–response session. A useful starting point is often to refer to school pupil profiles to see if any relevant information has already been shared. Alternatively, at the start of an academic year, you could ask for key information from pastoral staff, such as heads of year or tutors, on any pupils in your teaching groups about whom you should be aware.

- **Teacher–pupil relationship.** There will be times, especially at the beginning of the academic year, when relationships with pupils and teaching groups have not yet formed. The autumn term is the time to establish your classroom expectations and build rapport with your pupils. Even if you are an established member of staff, there might be individuals you have not taught before. They will need to get to know you and vice versa. This will inevitably mean that not all pupils will want to engage in asking or answering questions initially.

> **Pedagogy reflection:** Peer-to-peer relationships are often the biggest influence on pupil behaviour.

Research studies into classroom participation illustrate the significant role that a pupil's personality can have on their willingness to take part in lessons. Schunk and Pajares found that pupils with high self-efficacy were more likely to demonstrate higher academic achievement and participate more in the classroom.[6] Not only does their self-confidence tend to be higher, but they also know that contributing can benefit them by boosting their knowledge and understanding. They also demonstrate a higher

....

6   D. H. Schunk and F. Pajares, The Development of Academic Self-Efficacy. In A. Wigfield and J. Eccles (eds), *Development of Achievement Motivation* (San Diego, CA: Academic Press, 2002), pp. 15–31.

degree of self-regulation (we will explore this further in Chapter 4). These are often the pupils who have their hands up in lessons.

Activity

Pause for a moment and reflect on some of the pupils you teach. Are there certain pupils who always want to answer questions? What character traits do these pupils have?

Reflecting on my own classroom, I have found that pupils with low self-efficacy are reluctant to share their ideas. You can always tell by their facial expressions when you begin asking the class questions. I am convinced they are thinking 'Don't pick me! Don't pick me!' as my eyes scan the room ready to ask the next question. On the other hand, there are pupils who are desperate to answer your question or ask their own question. They shake and wave their hands to get your attention. These children want to share their thoughts, they want to be heard in the room and they want to please you. The disappointment when you don't pick them is all too obvious. Clearly, we don't want to burst their enthusiasm or willingness to contribute, but it is important that as teachers we set the expectations for classroom talk so that a small number of pupils don't dominate. (This is step 2 of how to build participation, which we will explore later on in this chapter.)

When initiating questioning in our classrooms, Mustapha and colleagues indicate that one of the reasons pupils are passive is self-limitation, such as being unable to focus, fear of offence or failing to demonstrate intelligence.[7] Alongside these factors, awkwardness and embarrassment can be amplified by peer pressure and the actions of the teacher. For example, calling on a pupil to

---

[7] S. M. Mustapha, N. S. N. A. Rahman and M. M. Yunus, Factors Influencing Classroom Participation: A Case Study of Malaysian Undergraduate Students, *Procedia Social and Behavioral Sciences*, 9 (2010), 1079–1084 at 1082. https://doi.org/10.1016/j.sbspro.2010.12.289

answer a question in front of their classmates can be daunting and shine an unwanted spotlight on them (just like my own experience as a pupil that I shared earlier). This led the researchers to conclude that fears relating to failure, peer pressure and the teacher's response all contributed to reducing pupil engagement and participation.

Equally, there will be other factors that may not be directly influenced by the school environment. Pupils with special educational needs and disabilities (SEND) may find it difficult to answer or ask questions. It is important for teachers to have a good understanding of the pupils we teach, so that if there are obstacles to participation then we can put in place suitable support strategies. On occasion, there will be pupils who won't be able to contribute an answer to a question publicly. Knowing this from the outset, before you teach the group, by reviewing pupil support plans is vital to avoid difficult situations that could impact on the pupil's mental health. Support plans will outline alternative strategies you could try to assist specific pupils with answering and asking questions.

The way we ask questions can have both a positive and negative impact on levels of participation. Getting the balance right between encouraging pupils to contribute and not embarrassing them is challenging. Our facial expressions and tone of voice when asking or receiving a question can give away our feelings too. Take a few minutes to consider how you behave when a pupil gives a wrong answer to a question. A negative reaction could impact on their willingness to answer further questions. This is one of the core principles of powerful questioning that I will outline in Chapter 5. Mustapha et al. also found that when the teacher was supportive during class discussions, through non-verbal gestures such as smiling when acknowledging a response, this fostered greater pupil participation.[8] There is a clear link between building confidence and active participation.

The importance of creating a questioning culture is not to be underestimated. One of the most challenging times of the year for

8   Mustapha et al., Factors Influencing Classroom Participation, 1081.

any teacher to establish this ethos, regardless of their experience, is the beginning of an academic year when we are assigned new teaching groups. The summer holidays create a gap of between four and six weeks in the normal routine of school life, so the autumn term is the time to instigate your classroom culture, get to know children you may have never taught before and realign pupils back into school customs and behaviours.

Even if you have encountered many of the pupils in the previous academic year, changes to groupings and pupils maturing as they move through the school can change the class dynamics. Despite these challenges, it is important to move our use of questioning forward to ensure it has an impact on our teaching and, ultimately, on pupils' learning. Taking the time to establish the norms in your classroom in the first few weeks of the new academic year are vital to setting up a positive classroom culture.

> **Pedagogy reflection:** Guided peer conversations can contribute towards supporting a collaborative learning environment.

Building participation

For teachers to use questioning as an effective pedagogic tool, a crucial starting point is building a conducive learning environment where there are interactions between teacher and pupils. In every classroom there are three core interactions: teacher to groups of pupils, teacher to an individual pupil and pupil to pupil. A conducive classroom environment will include all of these types of exchanges. The research indicates that teachers ask hundreds of questions a day,[9] but do these questions

---

9   L. Tamar and R. Long, *Effective Instruction* (Alexandria, VA: Association for Supervision and Curriculum Development), p. 20. Available at: https://files.eric.ed.gov/fulltext/ED200572.pdf.

promote interactions between teacher and pupil(s) instead of pupil-to-pupil discussions?

To improve knowledge retention, pupils need to be active rather than passive learners. There should be effortful engagement in a disruption-free environment. A silent classroom is a poor proxy for learning, but the assumption that a silent classroom equates to learning is still prevalent. Of course, there will be times when we want pupils to complete an independent task, and therefore it might be necessary for silence to ensure they remain focused. However, active engagement in the lesson is just as important to support learning and enable teachers to check for understanding. This means that we should expect pupils to be speaking to the teacher or their peers. Noise in a classroom is not an enemy to learning.

Without pupil participation, as a classroom practitioner you might as well be trying to use a crystal ball to guess what the pupils are thinking. In fact, Rosenshine indicates in his work on the principles of effective instruction that large amounts of pupil-to-teacher interaction promote and enhance pupil achievement over time: 'Students need to practice new material. The teacher's questions and student discussion are a major way of providing this necessary practice. The most successful teachers in these studies spent more than half of the class time lecturing, demonstrating, and asking questions.'[10]

However, there is a difference between compliant pupils and actively engaged pupils. Liu identified four types of pupil behaviours:

1. 'Full integration' – pupils 'engage actively' in the lesson and often 'know what they want to say and what they should not say'.

---

10   B. Rosenshine, Principles of Instruction, 14.

2. 'Participation in the circumstances' – pupils contribute at appropriate times, often influenced by socio-cultural factors, the environment and the relevance of the lesson.

3. 'Marginal interaction' – pupils act as listeners and rarely speak out in lessons.

4. 'Silent observation' – pupils tend to avoid any oral contributions in class.[11]

Consider one of your own teaching groups. I am sure there will be pupils who fall into one of these categories. As we have seen, factors such as peer pressure and fear of failure might be influencing the degree of pupil participation. So, as teachers, what can we do to build a classroom culture that will support all our pupils to achieve full integration?

> **Pedagogy reflection:** The more we ask the right questions, the greater the probability that this will promote and enhance achievement over time.

The following steps provide some guidance on how we might foster a strong classroom culture that will build the foundation for delivering powerful questions.

Step 1: Knowing your pupils

Picture the following scenario. You are about to pose an important question to the class, so you scan the room to decide who to ask, but you are not yet familiar with the pupils' names. You know that a particular pupil has answered a difficult question

---

11 J. Liu, *Asian Students Classroom Communication Patterns in US Universities: An Emic Perspective* (Westport, CT: Greenwood Publishing, 2001), cited in M. Y. Abdullah, N. R. A. Bakar and M. H. Mahbob, Student's Participation in Classroom: What Motivates Them to Speak Up?, *Procedia – Social and Behavioral Sciences*, 51 (2012): 516–522 at 517. Available at: https://doi.org/10.1016/j.sbspro.2012.08.199.

like this before and you have an inclination that they will know the answer, so you ask them: 'What do you think, err …?' Or, perhaps you have a number of pupils willing to share an answer to your question and you choose someone. After they have shared their response with the class you acknowledge, 'Excellent point, err …'

Not only is this an awkward situation to be in as the teacher, but it can be perceived negatively by the pupils too. Not knowing your pupils' names can have an impact on their levels of attention and willingness to contribute to class discussions. This was emphasised by Glenz, who said: 'A teacher that doesn't take the time to learn their students' names is often perceived as disinterested and unapproachable. By calling on a student by name, it gives the impression that the teacher cares about their success and develops a sense of trust.'[12]

One of the most difficult times for remembering pupil names is the start of a new academic year when you have a fresh set of teaching groups to navigate. If you have been at a school for several years, memorising the names of the pupils in front of you will probably be less demanding, but inevitably there will be times when you don't know some of the pupils in your class. If you are new to the school, getting to know your pupils will be one of the first challenges to building participation. Secondary school teachers not only have to remember the names of some 300 pupils a week, but there is also the added complexity of potentially having several pupils with the same name in the same class (e.g. Molly A, Molly D, Molly W). As school leaders, this is a factor we should be considering for our early career teachers because it is a hurdle that has to be navigated so early on in the profession. It is often just expected that teachers will be able to remember the names of their pupils.

··

12   T. Glenz, The Importance of Learning Students' Names, *Journal on Best Teaching Practices* (April 2014), 21–22 at 21. Available at: http://teachingonpurpose.org/wp-content/uploads/2015/03/Glenz-T.-2014.-The-importance-of-learning-students-names.pdf.

> **Pedagogy reflection:** Knowing your pupils helps to build classroom participation.

Ultimately, learning your pupils' names will help to create a receptive culture and develop positive relationships in your classroom. Research suggests that pupils make judgements about their teacher's credibility based on whether they can remember names.[13] It also increases pupils' confidence in their teacher. There are a number of strategies for remembering pupils' names, such as creating a seating plan with photographs or using cold calling as a questioning technique to get into the habit of using pupils' names right from the off.[14]

Step 2: Establishing expectations and building routines

Without the right routines there is no structure in our classrooms, and without structure talk will be harmed. From cutting across each other during class discussions to shouting out answers and not tracking someone who is speaking, a lack of routines will inevitably hinder learning. In order to foster a questioning culture, we need to explicitly teach and revisit the expectations for participating in asking and answering questions. Wong and Wong discuss a three-step approach to establishing expectations and building routines:[15]

---

13 Glenz, The Importance of Learning Students' Names.
14 Cold calling is described by Doug Lemov in *Teach Like a Champion 3.0: 63 Techniques That Put Students on the Path to College*, 3rd edn (San Francisco, CA: Jossey-Bass, 2021), technique 34.
15 H. Wong and R. Wong, *The First Days of School: How To Be An Effective Teacher* (Mountain View, CA: Harry K. Wong Publications, 2018).

1. Clearly *explain* the expectations and routines for classroom talk and why these are required and model these to pupils:

   - 'When contributing to a class discussion, it's important that only one person is talking at a time so that you can listen to their response.'

   - 'When contributing an answer to a question, remember to respond with clarity and in full sentences.'

   - 'There will be times when I want you to raise your hands before offering a response or I will choose someone to answer. I will signal what I'm expecting at a particular moment in the lesson.'

2. Give pupils plenty of opportunities to *rehearse* what you expect when participating in discussions:

   - 'Remember when someone is answering a question to track the speaker.'

   These regular nudges will help to build your routines so they eventually become part of your classroom habits.

3. Once expectations and routines are established, continue to *reinforce* these routines and narrate the positive to place a spotlight on what you expect when pupils participate:

   - 'Excellent tracking of the speaker, Tom.'

Pedagogy reflection: Establish the right conditions to foster classroom talk and regularly rehearse it so that pupils have opportunities to practise.

In *Atomic Habits,* James Clear discusses the temptation we might have to give up on establishing our expectations and routines. For example, Harry continually shouts out rather than putting his hand up to answer a question. After numerous attempts to reinforce your expectation that he puts his hand up when he wants to contribute, he continues to shout out multiple times each lesson. It would be easier to give up on reminding Harry about your expectations. Clear refers to this as the 'Valley of Disappointment'.[16] If we continue to explain, rehearse and reinforce our expectations and routines, then we will eventually hit a tipping point where we cross the valley of latent potential and the initial expectation and routine becomes a norm in the classroom.

If we don't spend the time rehearsing these routines and building social norms, Harry's repeated calling out can become a core attention distractor in your classroom. Other pupils will begin to resent Harry because he is impeding their ability to contribute. Furthermore, allowing Harry to shout out his answers signals to the class that this behaviour is acceptable in your classroom, leading to other pupils copying the behaviour. Explaining, rehearsing and reinforcing the expectations around classroom participation will need to be repeated to normalise your expectations and establish professional routines. It is worth acknowledging that it will be easier to reach some norms than others, but not giving up and continually accentuating them will lead to benefits for learning in the long term.

> **Pedagogy reflection:** Embedding routines is challenging. There will be times when you may feel that it isn't working. Give it time to embed, with lots of practice, and build in opportunities to review its success.

---

16 J. Clear, *Atomic Habits: An Easy & Proven Way to Build Good Habits & Break Bad Ones* (London: Random House Business, 2018), p. 22.

Step 3: Wait/think time

Filling the void after asking pupils a question is an art that teachers master over many years. There can be a tendency to answer the question before the pupil has responded rather than waiting and giving them time to think. I can think of numerous occasions when I have been asked a question and had very little time to consider my response, or the answer is on the tip of my tongue, when all of a sudden someone answers for me. Similarly, I have felt flustered when I have been rushed to reply. And, if I have been given a chance to answer but haven't had enough time to think about my response, I have ended up misconstruing the question or getting it wrong.

We all need some time to think about the question we have been asked. This is what Rowe referred to as 'wait time'.[17] There are two different types of wait time. The first is the amount of time a teacher waits from asking a question and the pupil responding, with research suggesting this is usually between three and five seconds.[18] The second is the amount of time the teacher waits once the pupil has stopped speaking before asking another question or continuing the lesson. When we give pupils the chance to think about their answer before responding, the more likely they are to give a more thoughtful response.

Not only does the research suggest that wait time can improve pupils' responses to questions, but Stahl also identified that wait time can be positive on teacher practice too. It makes their questions more varied and flexible, they reduce the number of questions and increase the quality and variety, and ask more questions that challenge pupils to use higher level thinking.[19]

17 Rowe, Wait Time.
18 P. Takayoshi and D. Van Ittersum, Wait Time: Making Space for Authentic Learning, *Kent State University Center for Teaching and Learning* (2018). Available at: https://www.kent.edu/ctl/wait-time-making-space-authentic-learning.
19 R. J. Stahl, Using 'Think-Time' and 'Wait-Time' Skillfully in the Classroom, *ERIC Digest* (1994). Available at: https://files.eric.ed.gov/fulltext/ED370885.pdf.

Rowe discovered that the wait time given to pupils following the teacher asking a question rarely lasted any longer than 1.5 seconds. The brief period between asking a question and waiting for an answer gives pupils little time to process the information and decide on how to respond. While Rosenshine indicated that the most effective teachers ask lots of questions,[20] without sufficient intervals between the questions it soon becomes a scattergun approach. Not giving pupils the space to think will quickly lead to questions becoming white noise in the room. Furthermore, expecting a fast response to a question will heighten the level of anxiety pupils feel in front of their peers. This can lead to the default response of 'I don't know', which we discussed earlier in this chapter.

What happens when we ask a pupil a question? There are numerous factors that the pupil will take into account before responding.

Firstly, they need to understand the purpose of the question. For example, a question like, 'What is hydraulic action?' will require a different response to, 'How does hydraulic action erode coastal landscapes?' The difference in the level of demand will affect how the pupil replies. Do they merely need to recall a key fact or figure, or are they expected to provide a more extended response? Secondly, the pupil needs to take into consideration their prior knowledge. Are they familiar with the subject matter? Can they work out the answer based on previous experiences or lessons? Thirdly, there is the anxiety of not knowing if the answer is correct and the potential embarrassment if they get it wrong.

All of these unseen factors from the simple act of asking a question! Therefore, giving pupils some breathing space between asking the question and expecting a response will allow them to process what they have been asked. So, how can we do this in the classroom?

---

20 Rosenshine, Principles of Instruction.

Consider the following question:

What is hydraulic action, Tom?

Once we have directed the question to Tom with no wait time, most pupils will have switched off because they know the question is for him.

Now, let's look at the difference when we ask the same question but in the following way:

What is hydraulic action ... (pause and scan the room), Tom?

In this instance, most pupils will be listening in the interval between asking the question and stating Tom's name because there is a possibility that we might come to them.

> **Pedagogy reflection:** Asking questions is complex and leads to an array of cognitive considerations for the receiver before they respond.

However, research from Rowe and others indicates that teachers rarely give pupils this time to think. In a study conducted by Hindman et al., the researchers observed the wait time in twenty-seven Head Start classrooms during shared book reading. They found that only one teacher provided pupils with any wait time, and this was only used a handful of times. They also reported that when the pupils didn't respond to a question within the first second of being asked, the teacher would follow up with a closed question or answer the question themselves.[21]

21 A. H. Hindman, B. A. Wasik and D. Bradley, The Question Is Just the Beginning: How Head Start Teachers Use Wait Time and Feedback During Book Reading. Paper presented at the annual meeting of the American Educational Research Association, New York, April 2018.

In a further experimental study by Hanna, teachers provided first-graders with wait time which resulted in the pupils providing more thoughtful answers and led to fewer non-explanatory 'I don't know' responses.[22] This suggests that giving pupils time to respond allows them to think about what they want to say and not feel rushed into giving a quick answer. However, as noted at the beginning of this section, introducing wait time before responding as a teacher is equally important to avoid the risk of cutting short a pupil's response.

So, what can we do to increase the use of wait time to promote active participation in our lessons? Here are a few strategies that could be implemented:

- Demonstrate what wait time means by modelling this to your pupils during class discussions. When asking a question, you might start by saying, 'When I ask you a question, I want you to think for a short time before giving me your answer.'

- Explicitly teach pupils how to actively listen to other contributors by asking them to track the speaker, so they can see how their peers use wait time before responding to a question.

- Be consistent in your approach and always remind pupils about using wait time. Explain the importance of taking some time to think about the question, which will allow them to respond with a more thoughtful answer.

> **Pedagogy reflection:** Allowing wait time creates the foundation for more thoughtful responses and encourages more pupils to answer questions.

....

22   G. P. Hanna, The Effect of Wait Time on the Quality of Response of First-Grade Children. Unpublished master's thesis, University of Kansas, KS (1977).

The powerful questioning classroom

Based on discussions from this chapter, in the table on the following page I have summarised what powerful questioning might look like for teachers and pupils when the right culture has been embedded in the classroom. This is by no means a definitive checklist – I may well have missed things that you think are good examples in your own classroom or school setting – but it does provide a blueprint when starting out with a new teaching group at the beginning of an academic year. How many of these are features in your classroom?

You may want to use this table as a guide to creating a classroom talk charter that you could work on with your pupils. Establishing what questioning looks like, and making regular references back to it, builds on Wong and Wong's three steps of explain, rehearse and reinforce. Involving pupils in this process can help to develop a powerful questioning culture because they feel they are part of the process and have a chance to understand the reasons why 'we do it like this in Mr Chiles' classroom' or 'we do it like this at Northwich Academy'.

Classroom culture
1. Asking and answering questions is a common feature of the classroom.
2. All contributions from teachers and pupils are seen as equally valuable.
3. Pupils feel confident about expressing their ideas without fear of sharing the wrong answer.
4. Time is provided to pupils when a question is asked to allow sufficient thinking time before responding.
5. How to ask and respond to questions are explicitly taught and modelled by the teacher.
6. Pupils are provided with regular opportunities to rehearse responses.
7. Pupils are encouraged to respond with full contributions when answering a question.
8. Peer-to-peer questioning is a common feature of class discussions.

Role of the teacher	Role of the pupil
Ask a range of question types.	Be prepared to answer questions.
Ask one question at a time.	Be curious and ask questions.
Give *all* pupils a chance to answer.	Allow others to answer and ask questions.
Allow wait time after asking a question and after pupils answer.	Listen to others answering and asking questions.
Allow pupils to ask their own questions.	Use wait time to consider answer before responding.
Encourage all pupils to respond to your question.	Ask for clarity when a question isn't clear.
Clarify question meaning when asked by pupils.	Track the speaker during a question–response session.

Activity

Take some time to reflect on the points in the table. How many of these are a common feature of your own classroom or setting? Do you spend time outlining them with pupils at the beginning of the academic year as well as at regular milestones during the year?

Have a go at creating your own powerful questioning charter with your pupils and share it with me on Twitter @m_chiles using #PowerfulQuestioning.

In the following case study, Catherine Owen, a geography subject lead, shares how she builds participation in her classroom to support a culture of questioning.

Case study: Building participation in a geography classroom

Catherine Owen

As an experienced teacher, it would be easy for me to slip into lazy habits in my classroom, so I read and engage with continuing professional development (CPD) to keep up to date with thinking in education and to keep myself challenged. Questioning is an area that fascinates me and in which I am always endeavouring to improve. When I identify an area I need to change in my practice or decide to integrate a new idea into what I do, I take small steps. I think carefully about the change I need to make – sometimes, I even note it down in an obvious place to remind me – then force myself to make the change repeatedly. I reflect upon whether the change is having the desired effect, then continue to repeat the changed behaviour until it becomes part of my natural practice. Only then will I introduce any further steps needed. In this way, I move from conscious incompetence through conscious competence to unconscious competence.

An example of this was breaking the habit of asking the question, 'Does everyone know what to do?' Very few pupils ever responded to this question with problems, leaving some to struggle. I made a decision to ask pupils to tell me what they understood by the task. Then, once I had built that habit into my repertoire, I developed it by 'bouncing' the question – asking other pupils if they agreed with the initial answer and if they could develop it. This had the desired result of pupils having far fewer problems with the tasks set.

Another area I needed to work on in the past was building participation in my lessons. At school as a pupil, I didn't speak in class unless addressed directly – and that happened very rarely. Catherine was the most common name in the year I was born, so when the teacher asked 'Catherine' to answer a question, I just kept my head down and another Catherine would usually answer. There were five Catherines in my GCSE French class!

When I started teaching, I was reluctant to put pupils on the spot – I knew how much I hated it – but I began to realise that allowing them to avoid participating was limiting their learning. My two-pronged approach to getting this right was knowing my pupils and having lots of tools for questioning at my disposal. If a pupil is going to be panicked by being asked a question, I might give them a note with the question on it at the start of the lesson, then call on them to answer it later on. If a pupil struggles to give an answer, I will allow them time to think. If they are still struggling, I may bounce the question to another pupil and then return to the original pupil to seek their opinion on the answer and ask if they can build on it. I tend to use a mixture of cold calling and hands up for questions – it is good to reward the enthusiasm of pupils keen to answer, but it is also important to draw in those less keen to participate.

I am terrible at remembering names, but I have overcome this problem with the help of technology. My school uses ClassCharts, so I have a seating plan for each class containing photographs and other information. Using names makes such a difference, as does really listening to pupils' answers. My school also has a clear behaviour policy, so if pupils jump in to answer questions, speaking over others, they are warned about their inappropriate behaviour. They are also rewarded for good behaviour for learning, such as answering questions – again using ClassCharts.

Remote teaching during lockdown brought new challenges in terms of questioning: during online lessons my pupils usually opted to have cameras off and were reluctant to speak. To avoid having to speak enthusiastically into the void for an hour, I had to think of strategies to engage pupils, whether through speaking out or typing responses in the 'chat box'. A key technique I adopted with my A level groups was waiting – even if the silence became a bit painful! I stopped myself from jumping in to answer my own questions and insisted on the pupils answering, refusing to move on until I had received contributions from them. I also used cold calling to good effect in this context.

Questioning will never be something I perfect; there are always aspects I can refine, new ideas to try out and new contexts in which I find myself working. This is why reading and participating in CPD are so vital. Working to improve our teaching doesn't only benefit our pupils; it also keeps us challenged, interested and engaged. It is exciting to think where my next steps to improve my questioning may take me.

Chapter summary and reflections

- Developing a culture where pupils want to answer and ask questions is not automatic and is fundamentally difficult. Reflecting on your own classroom, does it support a culture for powerful questioning?

- There will be times when accepting a non-explanatory response is easier because challenging pupils to respond can lead to more hassle. How can you build a culture so that pupils don't just give a non-explanatory response?

- Classrooms are dynamic environments, so there will be many factors affecting pupil participation, such as feeling shy, fear of failure and peer pressure. Spend some time getting to know your pupils and finding out about any individual SEND strategies that could be used to support them in asking and answering questions.

- Rehearsing routines can engage pupils in greater and more meaningful participation. How often do you narrate the routines in your classroom?

- When teachers ask a question, there is a tendency to answer the question before the pupils have had a chance to respond. What will you do to create a delay between asking and getting a response from your pupils?

- Expecting a fast response to the question can heighten children's nervousness about answering. What will you do to reduce pupils' anxiety when asking questions?

- Research demonstrates that when pupils don't respond to a question within the first second of being asked, the teacher will follow up with a closed question. To promote wait time, try modelling what wait time means, teach pupils how to explicitly track others speaking and be consistent in your approach to building routines.

- Develop a powerful questioning charter with your pupils or create a school-wide set of principles to establish what it looks like in your setting.

Now we have considered how we can foster a culture to enable powerful questions, the next chapter considers the role questions play in what I believe to be one of the most important elements of a lesson – checking for understanding.

Chapter 3

Questioning as a mechanism to check for understanding

Questions are powerful vehicles for processing information.

William Wilen[1]

In this chapter, we will:

- Reflect on the problems that can arise as a result of not regularly checking for understanding during the teaching and learning process.

- Unravel the importance of checking for understanding in the teaching and learning process.

- Consider the role of questioning as a tool to check for understanding.

- Look at how teachers can use questioning as a lever for responsive teaching through pedagogical strategies.

- Consider how to balance the use of information recall and higher order questions.

....

1   Wilen, *Questions, Questioning Techniques, and Effective Teaching*, p. 155.

Molly, a second-year geography teacher, is delivering a lesson to Year 9 on the processes that happen at plate boundaries. It is the final week of the half-term and she only has two lessons left with this teaching group before the holiday. Molly is very aware that she is already behind with the scheme of work compared to the rest of the department. She teaches the group the three plate boundaries with pupils annotating three diagrams. Towards the end of the lesson she asks the group, 'Do we all understand each of the boundaries? Does anyone have any questions?' to which none of the pupils respond. This is great, she thinks, because now she could move on to the next lesson, meaning she would be almost caught up with the rest of her colleagues.

Stuart is one of the Year 9 pupils in Molly's lesson. This is not the first time he has learned about plate boundaries, previously studying it in his Year 7 geography lessons. Some of the processes that Molly goes through are familiar to him, but there is a lot more detail that he needs to remember this time around. He annotates the diagrams with the key information, but he is struggling to keep up the pace and misses a few of the annotations on one of the diagrams. When Molly asks if everyone understands the boundaries, he wants to put his hand up, but he doesn't want those around him to know he isn't quite sure. He decides not to say anything and thinks he will check the next lesson.

I am sure we have all been there, like Molly, at some point in our teaching career. Getting through a scheme of work was almost an unwritten rule in the early stages of my own teaching career. If you weren't on track to complete the scheme of work by the end of the specified time frame, there were raised eyebrows at department meetings or questions asked about why you were behind. Back then, we spent very little time discussing the curriculum at meetings compared to now when it is the main focus.

It was as if we became obsessed with completing the curriculum rather than considering how we could deliver it effectively to the pupils and create the right conditions to promote effective learning. We were on a hamster wheel of curriculum coverage, ticking off each element of specification as if it was a checklist to success. Mary Myatt provides a powerful analogy that encapsulates this approach to content coverage, referring to it as 'Jackson Pollocking the curriculum'.[2]

On reflection, this approach was flawed because there is a fundamental difference between covering content and the pupils understanding it. The gap between delivery, understanding and retention of knowledge is blurry because the process of learning isn't neat and tidy. This unpredictability means that learning doesn't fit the logical narrative that many wish it did.

We shouldn't expect every pupil to be at the same point on the curriculum journey, and nor should we expect teaching groups to be neatly aligned across a department. After all, schools are dynamic environments, and the degree to which pupils understand our subjects is a moveable feast. This swinging pendulum of pupil understanding is impacted by an array of internal and external factors that we can't always control as teachers, no matter how hard we try and attempt to mitigate against them.

I want to reassure you that this is fine. It isn't something you should feel disheartened by and, more importantly, it shouldn't lead you to believe that you are failing your pupils. In my opinion, it is fundamentally wrong for schools to use time taken to cover the curriculum as a means to judge a teacher's capability. Inevitably, there are times when you will need to take a slightly different path for your pupils compared with your colleagues, or the pupils will need content to be retaught to cement their understanding. This is all part of the learning process. It is what many would

2   M. Myatt, Overrated: – Content coverage aka 'Jackson Pollocking the curriculum' Underrated: – Concepts aka big ideas, Twitter (27 July 2022, 9.54am). Available at: https://twitter.com/MaryMyatt/status/1552215754526920710?s=20&t= 6NMIdqwMSlTDNe0dbY7hrQ.

now refer to as being a 'responsive practitioner' through acknowledging that not every pupil in every lesson will instantly grasp what you have taught them. Teacher autonomy should be a prerequisite for curriculum delivery.

Pedagogy reflection: Learning is messy. We shouldn't expect every pupil to be at the same point on their learning journey. Look to support your pupils on their personal journey.

Activity

Take a moment to reflect on a time when you have needed to reteach something and answer the following questions: what did you have reteach? When did you have reteach it – the following lesson, several lessons or several weeks after the initial teaching? What prompted you to reteach it? How did it make you feel?

Teaching without being responsive to pupils' needs is a bit like setting off a new project and never reviewing whether it has been successful, merely leaving it to continue without any follow-up. Naturally, we need to evaluate our progress and determine if any changes need to be made to the original approach. The most successful teams continually review their progress and adapt as necessary along the way towards their intended goal. The same process should apply when we are teaching pupils; we have to build in time to review and reflect on their understanding. Equally, we should assess the effectiveness of the pedagogical strategies we have used to teach components of our curriculums. Without this evaluation, we might end up teaching a particular concept or process oblivious to the fact that it isn't being sufficiently understood by our pupils to enable them to apply it in different contexts.

In the early stages of my career, it was a badge of honour to be on track against the pre-planned curriculum schedule or ahead of other colleagues. Consequently, I have been guilty of falling into the trap of rattling through lessons. As long as I had covered each topic, I had done my bit as teacher – or so I believed. This never really sat right with me, but the pressure to keep up with colleagues was too all-consuming for someone new to the profession.

So, we carried on ploughing through the curriculum, ticking off each scheme of work as if it was an achievement. Of course, there were other external factors influencing the delivery of the curriculum – most notably, the pressure of getting through the GCSE specification in time for formal examinations. This meant that we would squeeze our curriculum delivery to meet an unwritten target of finishing the teaching of new content to Year 11 by Easter half-term. Why? Because this would give us time to get our revision lessons in before the main exams. When I look back at this time, I don't remember doing any recall of previously taught knowledge. We seemingly taught the curriculum in silos and expected the pupils to bring it all together at the end of their GCSE course.

Given everything we now know about learning, the idea of revision lessons was inherently flawed. While providing revision opportunities can be beneficial, we should be creating the expectation that revision is part and parcel of what pupils do right from the beginning of their studies, so they begin to develop scholarly habits that will support them for the future. Fail to do this, and pupils see revision as something they only do when working towards an internal or external examination. This sends out the wrong message around spacing their learning over cramming.

Spaced retrieval practice involves spreading learning events over regular intervals rather than trying to cram it into the period immediately before the test. Prior to acquiring an understanding of spacing, I would frequently ask pupils to complete a written assessment or end-of-topic test, which then led to a sea of unexpectedly poor attainment scores. This left me scratching my head as to why my pupils hadn't 'got it', as I had initially thought. I now know that although the curriculum had been taught, the knowledge hadn't been retained, so in fact it hadn't been learned at all.

> **Pedagogy reflection:** When teaching the curriculum, focus on reviewing pupil understanding over delivery, so that you can focus on closing knowledge gaps through reteaching where necessary.

Fast forward to today, and I no longer see getting through a scheme of work as part of my role as a teacher; instead, it is about making sure that my pupils have understood what I am teaching before moving on. Despite the pressures to 'cover' an exam specification or school-based curriculum, I spend far more of my time in lessons checking for understanding by revisiting prior and current knowledge rather than worrying about how much of the curriculum I have managed to get through in a half-term. What triggered this change in approach? The most significant driver was a growing awareness of cognitive science and how it can be applied in the classroom, which is slowly bridging the gap between research and everyday practice for teachers and school leaders.

However, there is a significant difference between knowing the research and using it effectively in your everyday practice. Of course, not every cognitive science approach will work every time, so you should always take into account the context of your own education setting. There can also be a tendency for research to be misunderstood when it arrives at the classroom door, leading to lethal mutations. Even when interventions are applied in the way they were intended, we have to accept that it takes time to implement new strategies in the classroom. This is something I have experienced with my own teaching. There have been times when I have tried a novel strategy, having read about it or seen someone else using it, and it doesn't work straight away. I could quite easily throw it out and say it doesn't work, but I don't. I spend time embedding it, reviewing it and tweaking it for my subject and school setting. After all, applying the theories of cognitive science isn't a one-size-fits-all approach.

For example, Rosenshine's principle of a daily review[3] combined with the learning strategy of retrieval practice is something in which I have invested time in my own classroom. When I initially introduced this as part of my routine, the pupils struggled to recall knowledge from memory and were reluctant to do so because it took them out of their comfort zone. I could have given in and allowed them to use their notes to find the answers, but this would have defeated the main objective of finding out what they could remember from memory and therefore what I needed to reteach or focus on in the lesson before teaching any new information. A few years later, the routine is now established and the pupils I teach have a clear understanding of the expectations and use the daily review as an opportunity to recall knowledge with higher levels of confidence. Of course, even after using this strategy for years, I still spend time revisiting the 'why' when I feel it is necessary and nudging the norms if pupils forget.

A second example is the use of grades, marks or percentages after a test or assessed task. In the past, I would have provided pupils with these prior to giving them any suggestions for improvements. Nowadays, I don't give them any marks for these pieces of work. Inevitably, pupils ask, 'What grade did I get?' or 'Who got the highest mark?' but I focus resolutely on the next steps for improvement and do exactly what I have done with the daily review strategy and nudging the norms when required.

Learning about cognitive architecture and cognitive load theory has provided me with an insight into the reasons why rattling

---

3   Rosenshine, Principles of Instruction, 13.

through the curriculum doesn't necessarily equate to effective learning. Of course, not everything was wrong with how I taught as an early career teacher because there were some pupils who did achieve their potential. However, it is likely that this approach neglected a large proportion of pupils who would have benefitted from spending more time reflecting on what they had been taught.

The more we try to unravel learning, the more complex it becomes. A multitude of factors contribute to its success. We know from cognitive science that learning happens when there has been a change in long-term memory. As teachers, we need to create regular opportunities to check that knowledge has been transferred and retained. This is why asking questions is a crucial mechanism for establishing whether what has been taught has been understood. We should see questions as the gateway to unlocking success. Learning is invisible, after all, and without knowing what pupils do and don't know, we can't act to redirect and help them to close knowledge gaps.

> **Pedagogy reflection:** Our role as teachers is to check what has been understood based on what has been taught.

Evolutionary psychologist David Geary categorised knowledge into two domains: biologically primary and secondary knowledge.[4] Biologically primary knowledge is the knowledge we have evolved to acquire over time – for example, learning to speak our native language or knowing how to interact with others. Biologically secondary knowledge is developed through information that we acquire by conscious effort – for example, learning about geography, maths or science. The key difference between primary

---

4   D. C. Geary, *The Origin of Mind: Evolution of Brain, Cognition, and General Intelligence* (Washington, DC: American Psychological Association, 2004).

and secondary biological knowledge is the effort it requires to learn it.

In the classroom, our core focus is on the acquisition of biologically secondary knowledge. Sweller highlights that the architecture of this information can be divided up into five key principles:

1. Generating novel information during problem solving

2. Obtaining novel information from other people

3. Working memory when processing novel information

4. Storing novel information in the long-term memory

5. Transferring familiar information from long-term to working memory to govern appropriate action[5]

Teachers and leaders have become increasingly aware of the role we play in supporting these principles when delivering the curriculum – in particular, the second principle of how we process and store information. When we are processing novel information, our working memory is limited, with an average person only able to hold approximately seven items of information[6] and process about three or four of these items.[7] We can only hold this in our working memory for a number of seconds without some form of rehearsal – the notion of 'use it or lose it'. Alongside this, how sticky this knowledge is will be dependent on our schema and whether we can forge connections from previously acquired knowledge. This understanding of cognitive architecture is vital to our knowledge of learning because our pupils are dealing with novel information on a daily basis.

5   J. Sweller, *Why Inquiry-Based Approaches Harm Students' Learning*. Centre of Independent Studies Analysis Paper 24 (August 2021), p. 6. Available at: https://www.cis.org.au/wp-content/uploads/2021/08/ap24.pdf.

6   G. A. Miller, The Magical Number Seven, Plus or Minus Two: Some Limits On Our Capacity for Processing Information, *Psychological Review*, 63(2) (1956), 81–97. https://doi.org/10.1037/h0043158

7   A. Renkl, Toward An Instructionally Oriented Theory of Example-Based Learning, *Cognitive Science*, 38(1) (2014), 1–37. https://doi.org/10.1111/cogs.12086

> **Pedagogy reflection:** When teaching new information to pupils, consider what prior knowledge they might have during your lesson planning.

Let's take the example of a typical Year 7 pupil who is going to five or six lessons a day, twenty-five to thirty lessons a week and covering up to eight different subjects. In each of these lessons, they will be grappling with new information, of which they may or may not have some pre-existing understanding and schemas. Perhaps Year 7 pupils are learning about cities in their geography lesson. Prior to starting this, they would probably have some basic understanding of cities from primary school through the Key Stage 1 and 2 curriculum. Alongside this, they may live in a city or have visited a city with their family, which would have enabled them to develop some awareness of their common characteristics. So, when a teacher introduces the term 'city', it will bring back some of these previously encoded experiences held in a schema in their long-term memory.

However, not all pupils will have had the same experiences, so their knowledge of cities will vary. This means that before starting to teach about urbanisation and the rapid growth of cities in the East in recent decades, the teacher would need to check that pupils are familiar with the concept of cities. After establishing whether this prior understanding is secure, the teacher would then determine whether they need to reteach any knowledge before moving on to the key learning intention for the lesson. This strategic check for understanding is an important element of the learning process to ensure that pupils' working memory isn't overloaded with new and unfamiliar information. Strategic questioning can provide a strong start to the lesson, and is a key mechanism in building up layers of information and developing pupils' subject knowledge.

Activity

Based on the previous scenario about cities, think of a topic you are going to be teaching this week and consider your answers to the following questions: what prior knowledge will the pupils need? How are you going to check the pupils have this prior knowledge? What misconceptions might the pupils have?

Pedagogy reflection: Periodically reviewing pupils' understanding and deciding on what needs to be retaught can help to reduce the burden of new and unfamiliar information on their working memory.

It could be argued that checking for understanding is the backbone of effective teacher instruction and should be a core feature of any teacher's classroom toolkit. Frequent check-ins throughout the lesson enable the teacher to ascertain what the pupils have understood in real time. The children's reactions will prompt a response from the teacher – a bit like when you arrive at a crossroads and need to make a decision on which route to take.

When you check for pupil understanding using questions, you are looking to affirm whether the information you have taught previously has been encoded and stored correctly, which will mean the pupils are able to recall this information as anticipated. When pupils are retrieving this encoded knowledge, you may uncover a misconception or gap. It is at this point that you have a choice to make: do you continue with the next layer of knowledge, or do you pause and reteach? This decision will be based on the field of responses you have gathered from your bank of questions.

Consider the following scenario. Sarah is teaching Year 7 about the themes in the poem 'Refugees' by Brian Bilston. Before they begin reading the poem as a class, she gathers information on their knowledge of palindromes. She asks them to spend one minute thinking independently about what the word means before writing it down and sharing it with the person next to them. After this quick recall activity, Sarah brings the class back together to check their understanding of the term. Depending on what she has discovered, Sarah can then decide whether she needs to spend some time explaining what a palindrome is before starting to read and analyse the poem with her class. Without this initial comprehension check, the pupils might not have understood the poem, which would mean that any analysis or follow-up activity based on it would have proved difficult for some children.

This is just one example of how retrieval practice can be used to check for understanding. In the following classroom snapshot, Alistair Hamill, a senior leader and head of geography, shares an insight into how he uses diagnostic questions to check for understanding in his classroom.

Classroom snapshot

Alistair Hamill

Geography takes theoretical models and applies them to real-world settings. I propose to take an example of one such application question I set my Year 13 pupils about plate tectonics. The question applies the model of plate movement to the Atlantic and Pacific oceans. The open-ended question asks the pupils to use evidence to explain differing rates of plate movement. The responses they make enable me to diagnose the extent to which they have understood the material enough to apply it. I set the task initially as homework for the pupils and then we discuss their answers in class. This allows me to assess their understanding and scaffold with further questions to help them, if necessary, move towards a fuller understanding.

Once we have done this, I give them another similar question but about a different ocean (the Indian Ocean). This again allows me to diagnose their developing understanding. Key through it all is to give them questions at the edge of their current understanding, to enable me to get feedback so we can progress further.

In the next section, we will consider several strategies that can help to check for understanding during the instruction phase.

Think, pair, share

Sarah's classroom scenario provided an example of how to use questioning as a means to check for understanding through the strategy of think, pair, share. The goal was to ascertain pupils' prior knowledge of palindromes before layering on new information. Think, pair, share was first developed by Frank Lyman in the 1980s. He referred to it as a cooperative three-step learning technique, which he believed provided pupils with an opportunity to think and increase communication and cooperation among peers. According to Lyman, there are four steps to the procedure of think, pair, share:

Step 1: A question is posed by the teacher to initiate the pupils to think.

Step 2: Pupils are given time to think actively about the question posed. The time allowed will depend on the complexity of the question – for example, a knowledge recall question will call for less time than a question requiring higher order skills.

Step 3:   Pupils discuss their thoughts in pairs.

Step 4:   Pupils are given the opportunity to share their discussions with the rest of the class.[8]

When you first use think, pair, share with your pupils, frontload the activity by explaining to them what it will involve and outlining what you expect from them at each stage of the process. Remember what we discussed in Chapter 2: creating the right culture when using questioning strategies is important to ensure that your pupils get the most from it. It may take several attempts before the pupils engage, but persevere with it. Each time you do think, pair, share, remind them of your expectations, which will help to nudge the norms for the strategy in your classroom and build strong routines.

One of the key benefits of using think, pair, share is that it gives pupils time to think about the question you have asked. So, after proposing the question in step 1, make sure you give the pupils plenty of time in step 2 to think independently. Kate Jones and Dylan Wiliam describe this as 'don't skimp on the "think"': 'When you pose a question to your class, the first impulse for students will be to turn and talk to a peer, skipping the thinking stage. Ensuring that ample think time is provided before the *pair* and *share* steps take place can prevent this impulse.'[9]

One of the key conditions for using the think, pair, share strategy as a tool to check for understanding is to keep it low stakes, which will reduce anxiety and enable pupils to attempt to recall what they might already know about the topic. The greater the stakes, the less likely pupils are to recall information, which means you won't find out what they do and don't know. Look to create the

8   F. Lyman, Think-Pair-Share: An Ending Teaching Technique, *MAA-CIE Cooperative News*, 1 (1987), 1–2.
9   K. Jones and D. Wiliam, Getting the 'Think-Pair-Share' Technique Right, *ASCD Blog* (13 October 2021). Available at: https://www.ascd.org/blogs/getting-the-think-pair-share-technique-right.

optimal conditions for promoting this independent recall – for example:

I'm going to ask you a question, and I want you to think about it by yourself before you discuss it with your partner.

Remember, we do this without our notes so you can try and recall it from memory. This might be challenging, but I want you to have a go.

Write down what you can remember on the whiteboard. Don't worry if you make a mistake. You can rub it out and start again if needed.

Encouraging pupils to work independently and from memory gives them the opportunity to think hard and engage in effortful retrieval practice. If you allow pupils to skip this initial think stage, they might just be repeating something their peer has recalled, depriving you of useful information about what they have retained. The checking for understanding would be pointless. Equally, if pupils refer back to their notes at this stage, it can give them a false sense of confidence about what they can remember, which doesn't help them to self-regulate or own their learning. Giving pupils this time to think also enables them to prepare what they want to say with their partner, reducing the anxiety of having to think on the spot in front of the class and the all too common non-explanatory response of 'I don't know'. This is emphasised by Raba in his research on the influence of think, pair, share: 'The more time they think about it, the fewer mistakes they make. In addition to that, it also gives the teacher the opportunity to check students' understanding and comprehension.'[10] If you don't provide this time, it is likely that pupils will struggle to engage in a productive dialogue during the share phase.

10   A. A. A. Raba, The Influence of Think-Pair-Share (TPS) on Improving Students' Oral Communication Skills in EFL Classrooms, *Creative Education*, 8(1) (2017), 12–23. Available at: https://www.scirp.org/journal/paperinformation. aspx?paperid=73454.

> **Pedagogy reflection:** Build pupils' confidence with recalling information from memory before seeking clarification or support from peers or from you as the teacher.

The amount of thinking time you give pupils will depend on the complexity of the question you have asked. Clearly, a higher order question will require pupils to take more time to process and recall information. Similarly, we need to give pupils plenty of time to write down their thoughts.

Prior to the pair phase, you could assign pupils as A or B and remind them to switch roles.[11] When first introducing this activity to your pupils, it might be helpful to model how to conduct this conversation; we shouldn't just assume that they will know what to do. Alongside modelling the discussion phase, you could also provide some question prompts to help them with their peer conversation. As the pupils gain in confidence, you can remove this scaffold.

Pressley suggests that step 2 of the think, pair, share strategy is important because it provides pupils with the chance to find out what they know and what they need to know.[12] Remind pupils to share with their partner what they have written during the thinking phase. If they have used mini whiteboards, encourage them to edit what they have written based on their discussion. When doing this activity for the first time, give pupils prompts to support their conversations. Towards the end of the allocated time, give them a heads-up when they should be drawing their discussion to a close, reminding them to be prepared to present their ideas: 'You have one more minute to discuss your ideas with your partner. Be ready to share your ideas with the rest of the group.' At this point you want all the pupils to feel they have an

11 Jones and Wiliam, Getting the 'Think-Pair-Share' Technique Right.
12 M. Pressley, Beyond Direct Explanation: Transactional Instruction of Reading Comprehension Strategies, *Elementary School Journal*, 92(5) (1992), 513–555. https://doi.org/10.1086/461705

opportunity to share their ideas or could be chosen to share their ideas.

> **Pedagogy reflection:** When using mini whiteboards, give pupils prompts on what success looks like so they have time to prepare their ideas before revealing them to you and their peers.

When it comes to the final step of sharing their answers with the rest of the class, ask individual pupils to describe their discussions. At this point of the lesson, you want all the pupils to be listening attentively with the understanding that you might call on them. Use the technique of cold calling to gather in their responses.

Mini whiteboards

We touched on the possibility of pupils using mini whiteboards to write down and share their ideas as part of think, pair, share. The key advantages of using mini whiteboards when asking questions include:

- They are very versatile and can be used with a variety of different activities, such as retrieval practice, planning answers, drawing and annotating diagrams.

- Pupils can easily erase their answer, so they are more likely to give it a go because they are not committing to an answer in their exercise books.

- A quick reveal of the whiteboards enables the teacher to quickly scan the room, identify any misconceptions and address them straight away.

- Teachers can see more than one response at a time.

- Pupils can try writing out a sentence, it can be checked by you and then they can commit to writing it in their exercise book.

- Pupils can spend time thinking about their response, enabling them to proofread and correct without fear of making a mess in their exercise book.

- Teachers can give instant feedback to dispel any misconceptions.

- Teachers can quickly spot non-participation and encourage pupils to contribute through supportive strategies.

> **Pedagogy reflection:** Mini whiteboards can be a powerful tool in encouraging greater participation in your classroom once scholarly habits are established.

To get the most out of mini whiteboards, it is important to establish a routine for their use when first introducing them to your pupils. This might include a countdown before all the pupils reveal their responses (e.g. '3, 2, 1 … show me your whiteboard') or pupils keeping their answers to no more than a sentence. Once these have become embedded, mini whiteboards will enable you to be a responsive teacher.

Consider the following scenario. Mark, a geography teacher, wants to check his pupils' understanding of key terms about river landscapes before moving on. Mark has modelled how to use mini whiteboards and established the routines he wants to see. Here are a few examples of how he uses mini whiteboards over a series of lessons.

Example 1: The pupils independently write an answer on their whiteboard with the aim of checking prior knowledge or the retention of knowledge.

Using your mini whiteboards, write down one factor that might cause river flooding to increase.

[Pause for pupils to write down their answers] …

Show me your answers in 3-2-1.

Example 2: The pupils work together to create an annotated diagram combining mini whiteboards with think, pair, share. They have previously been taught about how waterfalls form and watched a video to illustrate the processes. Prior to starting their drawings, Mark provides his pupils with success criteria and key vocabulary.

Using your mini whiteboards, I want you to independently draw an annotated diagram to illustrate the formation of a waterfall.

[Pause for pupils to draw diagram] …

Now, share your diagram with your partner. Use a green pen to add any extra detail that you might have missed initially.

Following on from this, the pupils would use the amended diagram to write an answer describing and explaining how waterfalls are formed.

Example 3: The pupils work independently to answer multiple choice questions written on the board.

Which of the following is the correct definition for hydraulic action?

1. The action of rock fragments colliding into each other and becoming smaller and rounder.

2. The sheer force of the water wearing away the bed and banks of the river channel.

3. The action of rock fragments scraping against the bed and banks of the river channel.

4. The action of the weak acidity of the river water wearing away the river channel.

On your whiteboard, write 1, 2, 3 or 4.

[Pause for pupils to write down their answers] …

Show me your answers in 3-2-1.

Mark scans the room to check the responses. He notices that a few pupils have selected the wrong answer, so he uses targeted questioning to dispel the misconceptions before moving on. He could have done this without the mini whiteboards, but cold calling or circulating the room might have taken longer. In this example, it was faster for him to use whiteboards to check for understanding.

Example 4: The pupils use their whiteboards to draft a response.

Mark has just taught his pupils new knowledge on river management, co-creating a memory map identifying the purpose, advantages and disadvantages of various soft and hard engineering techniques. He now wants them to apply this information by getting them to explain why a specific technique can help to manage a river. Mark models one example on the interactive whiteboard and then hands over to the pupils:

Right, now that I have modelled how to explain one type of river management, I want you to have a go at explaining a different one. Before you commit to writing an answer in your book, I want you to write out your explanation on your whiteboard. I'm going to give you a few minutes to do that.

Meanwhile, Mark circulates the room to check the pupils' explanations for their chosen management technique. He gives individual pupils some guidance on their explanatory sentence. When they are ready, he asks them to write a full answer in their exercise book.

As we can see from these four examples, there are many ways in which mini whiteboards can be used to promote classroom participation. The first step is getting the culture right so that mini whiteboards are used effectively to support the learning process.

In the classroom snapshot below, Richard McDonald, an assistant, shares how he uses mini whiteboards in his classroom.

Classroom snapshot

Richard McDonald

Initially, I didn't think mini whiteboards would work for class discussions in English, but the more I thought about my assessment of learning, the more I came across the issue that my sampling of pupils to check understanding was restricted to a small number, if I wanted to quickly assess knowledge within a lesson.

So, I turned back to mini whiteboards. Using these, I can see the whole-class response to a question and then use cold calling to probe responses further or find out whom I need to focus scaffolding strategies on later in the lesson.

The most important thing I have discovered, though, is to ensure that the logistics for this form of questioning are consistent and well rehearsed. I have found it useful to have whiteboards out on desks for all lessons, as it means there is no need to hand them out (pupils also need to have their own pens/erasers).

When it comes to routines, I have used the WalkThrus 'show-me board' approach across the school.[13] Reinforcing staff CPD through deliberate practice with pupils (e.g. through quiz activities in form time) made for an approach that was adopted across the school. I particularly like how practical subjects can use the same routine with hand signals (e.g. one to five fingers for multiple choice questions and thumbs up/down for true/false).

Activity

Reflecting on the scenarios in Mark's and Richard's classrooms, consider the following questions on the use of mini whiteboards with colleagues in your department: how could you use mini whiteboards in your subject? What might you do to establish scholarly habits when using them? What type of activities would work for your subject?

In the next classroom snapshot, Jo Blackman, assistant head of teaching and learning/head of design technology, provides a glimpse into her classroom to share how she uses technology as a tool to ask questions that check for understanding.

---

13   T. Sherrington and O. Caviglioli, *Teaching WalkThrus: Five-Step Guides to Instructional Coaching, Vol. 1* (Woodbridge: John Catt Educational, 2020).

Classroom snapshot

Jo Blackman

In my context, pupils have a one-to-one device as I find it powerful to outsource technology to achieve quick questioning wins. Nearpod and Microsoft Forms enable me to offer whole-class multiple choice questioning, matching pairs or sorting tasks. These low-stakes activities build confidence and start the discussion. We then review peers' work and model improvements and, finally, ask more high-order questions using a mixture of cold calling, think, pair, share and hands up as the complexity builds. If pupils give me a short response, my favourite follow-up is, 'Good start, can anyone build on this?' which leads to more fruitful contributions.

Without putting in the low-stakes groundwork, using retrieval practice as a vehicle to revisit information they already know as scaffolding, questioning is not as effective. By using a variety of strategies, which then get woven into the discussion, without knowing it pupils get swept up in the journey of the content we are exploring.

On the flip side, it is worth noting at this point that moving on when knowledge isn't secure (through strategies like think, pair, share and mini whiteboards) may have a negative impact on pupils' ability to encode new knowledge. It is a bit like trying to build a house on weak foundations: there is a high probability that it won't be standing strong some years later. (Think back to the scenario on teaching cities and the example you reflected on relating to your own subject.) Psychologists describe memory as having three distinct stages: encoding, storage and retrieval.[14] As teachers, we need to check on a regular basis whether pupils'

14 S. A. McLeod, Stages of Memory: Encoding Storage and Retrieval, *Simply Psychology* (5 August 2013). Available at: https://www.simplypsychology.org/memory.html.

knowledge is secure and has been encoded correctly. Are they able to remember the information over time and use it in different parts of the connected curriculum?

Clarifying mistakes vs errors

The decision about whether to set pupils off on independent practice or pause and reteach is challenging. There is no silver bullet because, as we have seen, learning isn't a neatly organised process. There will be times when you won't need to spend too long revisiting previously taught information before moving on, and other times when you will need to reteach the same material several times.

This decision will be influenced by evidence of pupils' mistakes or misconceptions. Fisher and Frey suggest that mistakes often occur due to a lack of attention caused by fatigue or peer distractions.[15] As a teacher, you can determine whether a pupil has made a mistake due to faulty knowledge recall because you will have an awareness of what they could recall in previous lessons. Another way you might be able to tell if a pupil has made a mistake is when they correct themselves by saying, 'Actually, I meant to say …'

Fisher and Frey submit that pupils make four different types of error during lessons:

1. *Factual errors* affect pupils' ability to use knowledge with accuracy. For example, in geography, pupils might recall the difference between saltation and traction incorrectly. If you identify that a pupil has made a factual error, you can reteach to correct the misunderstanding.

---

15   D. Fisher and N. Frey, *Checking for Understanding: Formative Assessment Techniques for Your Classroom*, 2nd edn (Alexandria, VA: Association for Supervision and Curriculum Development, 2014).

2. *Procedural errors* occur when pupils struggle to apply factual information. For example, pupils might know the process to calculate the mean value from a data set but they make an error by not dividing the total value by the number of values. You might spot this during guided practice as you circulate the room.

3. *Transformation errors* happen when pupils choose to use the same process in different scenarios. For example, they might learn a term in several subjects but the meaning is different: in English, the concept of evaluating can mean to give your personal opinion but in geography it might mean to evaluate the evidence provided.

4. *Misconception errors* transpire when pupils misconstrue what they have been taught. For example, in science, they may believe that all bacteria are bad when, in fact, many protect the body from infection.[16]

This is why building a culture of learning, where attention is a core component of lessons, should be at the forefront of effective teaching instruction, and also why checking for understanding is a critical part of the learning process. Think, pair, share, mini whiteboards and cold calling can all help to uncover areas where pupils are struggling and what knowledge needs to be retaught.

Unfortunately, there is no magic number or percentage for how many pupils should have understood what you have taught before you move on with the next layer of knowledge. However, if you only gather responses from a small number of pupils, then you are unlikely to have a broad picture of their understanding. Dylan Wiliam and Paul Black reflect on this issue in *Inside the Black Box*: 'The teacher, by lowering the level of questions and by accepting answers from a few, can keep the lesson going but is out of touch with the understanding of most of the class.'[17] An over-reliance on one strategy, such as cold calling or hands up,

---

16 Fisher and Frey, *Checking for Understanding*, pp. 4–5.
17 P. Black and D. Wiliam, *Inside the Black Box: Raising Standards Through Classroom Assessment* (London: GL Assessment, 1998), pp. 11–12.

might lead to teachers only selecting and accepting answers from a restricted number of pupils, potentially skewing their understanding of what the class know, what they have remembered and what they can do with the knowledge they have been taught.

> **Pedagogy reflection:** Checking for understanding should be happening throughout the lesson to give you the ammunition to be a responsive teacher.

Reflecting on what we have discussed so far in this chapter, when teachers regularly check for understanding it allows them to do the following:

- Check what pupils currently do and don't know.

- Gather information to decide whether to move on, slow down or reteach.

- Review the depth of prior knowledge, which enables you to know what needs to be retaught before new knowledge is introduced.

- Check the retention of knowledge from previous learning experiences.

- Discover the extent to which pupils may have embedded misconceptions.

- Reduce the potential of pupils practising and reinforcing previous mistakes.

- Encourage pupils to become more aware of how to monitor their own learning.

Activity

Pause for a moment and think about a recent lesson where you have used questioning to check for understanding: what questions did you use? Did you decide to move on from this check, or did you conclude that you needed to reteach information? What prompted you to make this decision?

Now that we know what we mean by checking for understanding, we should also consider what checking for understanding is not and where it is not used as effectively as it could be. I am sure we have all had an experience like this in our teaching careers: we deliver what we deem to be a brilliant explanation and, as we are about to set our pupils off on some form of independent practice, we say: 'Okay, does everyone understand?', 'Does that make sense?' or 'Does anyone have any questions?' The pupils remain silent, leading you to believe that they understand. However, at the end of the lesson, when you check through their books, their lack of comprehension is all too apparent.

The silence in the room has given you a false sense of what has been understood. It is human nature not to want to admit in a room full of people that you don't get something. As we discussed in Chapter 2, there are various interrelating factors that will affect whether pupils are prepared to be honest – most notably, the fear of failure or embarrassment in front of their peers. Therefore, in this first example, checking for understanding is not merely about asking a question like, 'Does that make sense?' because it is unlikely to elicit the answer you want. When we check for understanding, our goal is to reduce the gap between what has been taught and what has been learned. Asking 'Does that make sense?' might lead to some pupils answering honestly that it doesn't, *if* the classroom culture is strong. However, you are not really checking *what* has been understood. The question represents a superficial check for understanding and is far too broad. A more effective method would be to ask directed questions that check what pupils have genuinely understood using mini whiteboards, think, pair, share or a retrieval quiz.

Consider the following scenario. Rachel, a history teacher, wants to check if her pupils have understood the key events around the Battle of Hastings before she sets them off on an independent writing task. She prepares a series of specific knowledge recall questions to check if their understanding of this event is secure. The first question is: 'Where did the Normans land in England?' This will check whether they remember the challenges William faced when attempting to cross the Channel. If their answers indicate that the knowledge isn't secure, she can reteach this material before they begin their written task.

We should also consider how long we allow between teacher instruction and checking what has been learned. For example, we wouldn't rely on final exams or external tests to check for pupils' understanding because by then it is too late to do anything about it. Similarly, we shouldn't leave it too long between episodes of retrieval, which could lead to misconceptions becoming embedded and taking longer to be dispelled. Knowledge can become fragmented if pupils don't revisit it for long periods of time. This means that when they do try to recall knowledge and apply it in a high-stakes test, they often perform poorly. This is why summative assessments are unhelpful in checking for understanding.

In my experience, high-stakes summative assessments are best deployed to determine whether a pupil is on track in terms of their expected progress or target grade after an extended period of instruction. Equally, the measures used to determine progress against targets are all too often flawed, with summative assessments not always reflective of a typical external examination. Therefore, a distorted picture is generated of what has been learned and understood. The whole idea of creating opportunities to check for understanding during instruction is so that you can act on the information you receive, allowing you to be a more responsive teacher. You find out what your pupils know and don't know, enabling you to plan what to do next.

> **Pedagogy reflection:** Regular opportunities to check for understanding allow you to determine what has been understood and to respond as necessary.

Over the past fifteen years, I have had the privilege of watching colleagues teach. Inevitably, there have been occasions when the teacher has missed an opportunity to check for understanding before moving on with instruction. Unsurprisingly, once the pupils have been tasked with some form of practice, hands go up and the teacher is frantically moving around the room and reaffirming expectations. I suspect this scenario may resonate with many teachers because we commonly make the assumption that pupils have followed the information delivered during the instruction phase.

As Schmoker observes: 'an enormous proportion of daily lessons are simply never assessed – formally or informally. For the majority of lessons, no evidence exists by which a teacher could gauge or report on how well students are learning essential standards.'[18] In a study by Vosniadou et al., two groups of students took part in a physics lesson. One group had their understanding checked before moving on to the next part of the lesson, while the other group didn't have any pauses to check for understanding. The researchers found that the first group demonstrated higher scores on the tests.[19]

....

18 M. Schmoker, *Results Now: How We Can Achieve Unprecedented Improvements in Teaching and Learning* (Alexandria, VA: Association for Supervision and Curriculum Development, 2006), p. 16.

19 S. Vosniadou, C. Ioannides, A. Dimitrakopoulou and E. Papademetriou, Designing Learning Environments to Promote Conceptual Change in Science, *Learning and Instruction*, 11(4–5) (2001), 381–419. https://doi.org/10.1016/S0959-4752(00)00038-4

We will explore the role of diagnostic and reflective questions based on an assessment model over a series of lessons in Chapter 4, but first we will consider how, after checking for understanding, probing questions can be used to activate hard thinking, moving pupils from lower to higher order thinking.

Probing questions to deepen understanding

Once you have used questions to check for understanding, you might then want to use probing questions to get pupils to think more deeply. As we have seen, the level of pupils' thinking is determined to a large extent by the questions teachers ask. We know from the research in Chapter 1 that all too often these questions are at a lower cognitive level. Once we have developed a strong culture in our classrooms and an understanding of question typology, the challenge is how we use them to extend pupils' thinking beyond initial recall.

In his study of elementary classrooms, Mehan identified that the basic form of instruction is the initiation-response-evaluation (IRE) mode.[20] Teachers ask a question, a pupil responds and then we evaluate the response. At face value, this framework can appear restrictive, with the response and evaluation part remaining a brief exchange that merely recalls knowledge or affirms the response the teacher expected. However, with careful thought, the evaluation element offers a great opportunity for teachers to present another question and build an extended response by offering *feedback*, and in so doing changing IRE to IRF.

The follow-up feedback, with additional probing questions, has the potential to initiate deeper reasoning from pupils through questions that use thinking operations like explain, assess,

....

20 H. Mehan, *Learning Lessons: Social Organization in the Classroom* (Cambridge, MA: Harvard University Press, 1979).

consider and evaluate. This extension of the IRF discourse was analysed by van Zee and Minstrell, who studied its effectiveness in a physics lesson. The focus was on the feedback element, referred to as the 'reflective toss', where a teacher asks a follow-up question and puts the thinking back on to the pupils. The researchers found that this had the following benefits: it made the pupils express their meanings more explicitly, consider a variety of other pupils' views and prompted pupils to reflect on their own views.[21]

Throughout this chapter, we have considered how questions can be a mechanism to check for understanding and to support learning and the retention of knowledge over time. We have explored how it might be used ineffectively and the role of probing questions in deepening understanding. To illustrate how questioning can be applied more widely, Stuart Pryke, an assistant principal and English teacher, provides a glimpse through the keyhole of his classroom to share how he uses questioning as a tool for responsive teaching.

Case study: Responsive questioning in the English classroom

Stuart Pryke

English as a subject allows us to explore, navigate and consider the human condition through time; it lets us scrutinise the many forms and functions of our language, both positive and negative; and it can empower pupils to think about how writers use it to promote their ideas about the way we live to the world. In short, it is a commentary on what it means to be human.

....

21   E. van Zee and J. Minstrell, Using Questioning to Guide Student Thinking, *Journal of the Learning Sciences*, 6(2) (1997), 227–269. https://doi.org/10.1207/s15327809jls0602_3

When it comes to the articulation of ideas in English, then extended written responses are vital not only in demonstrating key understanding of a writer's ideas but also in allowing pupils to 'deep dive' into the minutiae of plot, theme and character. Extended responses allow for originality and creativity; they are a chance for our pupils to contribute their own valuable voices to literary discourse. In encouraging pupils to extend their ideas, we are telling them that their opinions, ideas and voices matter. They should be heard.

However, extended written responses can be met with reluctance. For some pupils, essays are intimidating, threatening and made up of a series of deceptively intricate components that they must master in order to write with success.

Let's consider a commonly phrased extended question in English: 'Explain how X uses language to present Y.' In my experience, pupils are often good at explaining what a writer wants to do and how they do it but neglect why they do what they do. In encouraging pupils to extend their responses, I will often conduct what I call 'the why test', which involves skimming and scanning an answer and simply writing 'why?' next to each part that isn't yet perceptive enough. Letting pupils puzzle over a question is important; I sometimes think we are too keen to give them the answers. In some cases, I may help some pupils by saying, 'Explain to me why this is the case using the words X, Y and Z in your response,' but, ideally, an extended response is about hearing a pupil's own thoughts, not those I have imposed upon them.

James Britton observes how 'reading and writing float on a sea of talk'.[22] Oracy is key to helping pupils extend their written responses. What I love about English as a subject is how it lends itself so well to probing questions. There is always

....

22 J. Britton, Writing and the Story of the World. In B. M. Kroll and C. G. Wells (eds), *Explorations in the Development of Writing: Theory, Research, and Practice* (New York: Wiley, 1983), pp. 3–30 at p. 11.

another interpretation to explore, symbolism to elucidate and authorial intent to dissect. A wealth of debate lurks in the words we study. Encouraging pupils by questioning them further on their ideas is a great way to tease out extended responses. Probing questions require pupils to articulate their ideas beyond their initial answer, to contemplate ideas and proposals they may not necessarily agree with, and to digest these comments in order to think about alternative points of view. I ask probing questions because I think the idea that 'there's not really a wrong answer in English' is an unhelpful one; we should be interrogating answers offered, challenging them and making pupils think rather than accepting the first thing they say. Probing questions I tend to ask include:

- Are you sure?

- What might someone who disagrees with that interpretation say?

- Can you explain to me why you came to that conclusion?

- Can you say that again, but say it better using the words X, Y and Z?

- What evidence is there to support what you are saying?

The power of these questions can only really be appreciated when placed in context. For example, if my original question is, 'Has Scrooge really changed by the end of *A Christmas Carol*?' a pupil may reply alongside the lines of, 'Yes, he has changed because he demonstrates his newfound benevolence through his actions towards Bob Cratchit, Fred and the charity gentlemen.' I may dig a little deeper with, 'What are these actions?' but in doing this, I am only checking their knowledge of the text (which is important too!) rather than eliciting a more exploratory response. Asking, 'What might someone who disagrees with this interpretation say?' forces this pupil to stop and reconsider their initial thoughts. In navigating this new idea, pupils effectively rehearse, through talk, the multiple interpretations I would want to see in an extended piece of writing. Talk allows pupils to prepare, practise and go over what they need to write. It decreases the threat of committing their viewpoints to paper.

Chapter summary and reflections

- There is often a gap between the delivery, understanding and retention of knowledge because the process of learning isn't neat and tidy.

- We shouldn't expect every pupil who is following a curriculum to be at the same point on their journey, and nor should we expect teaching groups to be neatly aligned across the department.

- Teacher autonomy should be a prerequisite for curriculum delivery. How can you work with your colleagues to plan collaboratively?

- There is a growing hunger to explore and reflect on how research can be applied in the classroom, which is slowly bridging the gap between the research and everyday practice for teachers and school leaders.

- Our role as teachers is to create regular opportunities to check that knowledge has been transferred and retained. What strategy could you adopt next lesson to build in opportunities to use questions to check for understanding?

- Questions are the gateway to unlocking success. Learning is invisible, and without knowing what pupils know and don't know, we can't act to redirect and help them to close knowledge gaps.

- Questioning is an important mechanism enabling teacher and pupil to check that knowledge has been encoded and understood.

- Develop scholarly habits prior to using mini whiteboards to improve question participation.

- Avoid reliance on a single strategy, such as cold calling or hands up, because it can lead to teachers only selecting and accepting answers from a restricted number of pupils, resulting in a distorted view of what has been understood.

In this chapter, we have considered the role of questioning in supporting teachers to check for understanding. In the next chapter, we will consider how questioning can be used to diagnose and reflect on learning.

Chapter 4

Diagnostic and reflective questioning

In this chapter, we will:

- Explore the role of questioning as a tool for assessing learning.

- Consider how to create powerful questions to diagnose performance.

- Explore how the use of questions can support pupils to become more reflective learners.

- Review the role of metacognitive talk in the classroom to build self-regulation habits with pupils.

- Look at how questions support the process of mentoring in schools for both teachers and pupils as a reflective tool.

1   I. Gandhi, *Speeches and Writings* (New York: Harper & Row, 1975), p. 147.

Bartise is a science teacher working in a secondary school in the South East of England, which is focusing on a new assessment model. In recent CPD sessions, the key message for him and his colleagues has been the importance of getting assessment right in order to diagnose performance. The focus is on using the data to close knowledge gaps and not on marks or percentages per se. In recent weeks, Bartise has been planning questions with his science colleagues, but in practice he is finding that the questions he asks are not always revealing pupils' knowledge gaps or misconceptions. Bartise reflects on the questions that were asked to his Year 7 pupils for a previous assessment, as he knows that asking the right questions is crucial to identifying knowledge gaps and acting as a responsive teacher.

Penny is an English teacher working in a secondary school in the North West of England. The school expects teachers to use high-stakes summative assessments via end-of-topic tests to track pupils' progress towards their target grade. The tests focus on isolated aspects of knowledge that aren't revisited. The marks are recorded, and Penny discusses with her head of department those pupils who are not on track. Not only does the regular collection of marks every six weeks add to Penny's workload, but she also questions the value of these summative assessments. They tell her little about what her pupils have learned and where their knowledge gaps are because the focus is on how well they have performed against the benchmark set. Penny believes that assessments should be used to improve learning, not prove learning.

Formative and summative assessments

Establishing an effective process to assess learning is one of the biggest challenges for schools, leaders and teachers to get right. Choosing the wrong assessment model can create extra workload for teachers like Penny and stress for her pupils, but this doesn't need to be the case when designing a model for individual school contexts. Instead, school leaders should work with colleagues to support and enable teachers to use assessment as a mechanism for closing gaps in their subjects. Frequently, assessments are used to check teacher performance rather than how well pupils have learned the curriculum. They are used to prove that learning has taken place rather than to improve learning.

Let's consider some examples of how we might measure how well pupils are learning in our lessons using retrieval quizzes, extended writing (like essays), homework tasks and formal exams. All of these different assessment methods can be used formatively and summatively.

To illustrate this, we can use the metaphor of a train ride. Summative tests represent the end of that journey – the final stop. They are a formal assessment of how much has been learned. Conversely, when assessment is used formatively, pupils get on and off the train as directed by their teacher, through regular informal testing, which is followed up by written and verbal feedback on how to get to the end of their journey.

Potentially, formative assessment can have a bigger impact on learning and, in turn, pupil progress. Equally, using assessment for formative purposes means we can review the success of the pedagogical approaches used to teach pupils what we want them to learn. From this, we can adapt our approach to how the curriculum is taught.

When schools place a greater emphasis on high-stakes assessment models for summative purposes, it inevitably means that teachers like Penny focus on ensuring that outcomes reflect internal data targets and benchmark expectations. As a result, data collected from the assessments don't always provide the necessary information to help teachers or their pupils, meaning that assessment shifts even further away from evaluating gaps in pupils' knowledge and their ability to apply aspects of the curriculum.

The use of level-based and benchmark assessments can create a distorted picture of what pupils know and understand, ultimately impeding their progress over time. This is compounded by the emphasis on high-stakes summative over low-stakes formative assessment, as emphasised by Fletcher-Wood: 'Assessments for summative purposes dominated my teaching, my leaders' expectations and my students' thoughts: this hindered learning.'[2] However, there will be times when we want to gather information about the pupils' broader understanding of the curriculum, covering a wider range of knowledge and skills from over a longer period of time.

Activity

Reflect on your current school's assessment model. What is the balance between the use of assessment for formative and summative purposes? Do you think your current approach to assessing learning is effective?

---

2   H. Fletcher-Wood, *Responsive Teaching: Cognitive Science and Formative Assessment in Practice* (Abingdon and New York: Routledge, 2018), p. 4.

Cumulative diagnostic assessment

In Chapter 3, we explored how questions can be used to check for understanding during lessons, but there will be times when we want to capture what pupils have learned through more structured means. Diagnostic assessments might look at pupils' retention of knowledge over time as well as their understanding of how to apply it in different subject disciplines, and can be both formative and summative.

The role of questions is a crucial cog in the assessment process because they will essentially determine what we do as teachers to close knowledge gaps, either through feedback or probing follow-up questions. If the questions we ask don't effectively reflect the curriculum taught, the information produced will be of limited use in moving the learning forward; therefore, getting the questions right is fundamental. As discussed in the previous chapter, we can use a variety of question types to check for understanding before moving the learning on, revisiting content or addressing misconceptions. As a responsive teacher, these are all important moments in our classroom for guiding learning.

> **Pedagogy reflection:** Formative assessments provide greater opportunities for teachers to be responsive and plan the next steps to promote learning and retention over time.

This leads us on to how schools can create assessment opportunities that use a broad range of question types to cumulatively build new knowledge over time. In the past, I have worked in schools where pupils have completed end-of-unit tests after a block of lessons. These summative tests treated knowledge in isolation, reviewing what the pupils had understood from a unit of work on, for example, the Battle of Hastings in history. The test usually takes place many weeks or months after the pupils were taught the material. If the teacher has provided few opportunities for them to revisit previously taught knowledge, then it is no surprise that the pupils performance didn't always reflect what they had demonstrated in lessons. Structured high-stakes summative assessments tend to yield high teacher workload, but low impact in terms of supporting teachers to understand what their pupils know and how to move the learning forward. As Black and William observe: 'for formative purposes, a test at the end of a block or module of teaching is pointless in that it is too late to work with the results.'[3]

And when teachers sit down to mark summative tests, often the information they provide isn't enlightening. This creates a challenge for school leaders and teachers when seeking to develop assessment models that accurately review what pupils have learned. Although pupils may perform well in an end-of-topic assessment, this doesn't mean they have learned the concepts and processes. This is all too evident when, some months later, they end up struggling to recall and apply these same concepts and processes in another summative assessment. We know from extensive research into how the memory works that there is a difference between learning and performance. Learning takes place when there is a change in long-term memory, while performance is what we can observe and measure in the short term. Therefore, success in one assessment is not a reliable indicator that learning has actually occurred. For this reason, summative assessments, through methods such as mock exams, should be used infrequently.

In contrast, cumulative diagnostic assessments involve frequent and interspersed testing. This approach allows teachers to devise structured interim assessments that weave and build in knowledge from previous parts of the curriculum. It cultivates the right conditions for pupils to revisit knowledge and concepts from topics over time, strengthening schema and deepening their understanding of the subject. It is supported by Popham's

---

3   Black and Wiliam, *Inside the Black Box*, pp. 12–13.

work on learning progressions, which he defines as 'a carefully sequenced set of building blocks that students must master en route to mastering a more distant curricular aim. These building blocks consist of subskills and bodies of enabling knowledge.'[4]

With this in mind, one approach to using questions to assess learning over the course of an academic year is cumulative diagnostic knowledge quizzes, which evaluate whether pupils remember the nuts and bolts of the subject content they have been taught. Quizzes should be structured using three core components: current knowledge, prior knowledge and explicit subject vocabulary. The type of questions used can be open response (free recall) or multiple choice.

Open response questions will require pupils to think harder because of the lack of plausible prompts. Lemov and Jones observe: 'Free recall questions generally require more effort – more "desirable difficulty" from students to answer. This is because recall – remembering something without a cue – is harder than recognition – which requires knowing, selecting and identifying the right answer when you see it.'[5] Open response questions allow pupils to demonstrate wider knowledge when there are options available for them to provide a full answer, while multiple choice questions can be used to determine common misconceptions by including credible distractors.

When devising diagnostic tests for cumulative assessment, the aim is to create questions that promote more than just the reciting of facts and details. The tests should include enough challenge to make the pupils think and provide an insight for you as their teacher into their progress in your subject.

....

4   W. J. Popham, All About Accountability: The Lowdown on Learning Progressions, *EL*, 64(7) (2007). Available at: https://www.ascd.org/el/articles/the-lowdown-on-learning-progressions.

5   D. Lemov and K. Jones, On Hybrid Question Design in Retrieval Practice, *Teach Like a Champion* (14 September 2021). Available at: https://teachlikeachampion.org/blog/on-hybrid-question-design-in-retrieval-practice-with-kate-jones.

> **Pedagogy reflection:** Create knowledge quizzes with a range of open response and multiple choice questions to prompt deeper thinking.

Reflective questions

In the first part of this chapter, we explored how questions can be used as a diagnostic tool to provide guidance on how well pupils have learned the curriculum. We now shift our focus to how questions can be used to prompt pupils to reflect on their learning. Before we unpick this further, consider the two scenarios of pupils Thomas and Chloe:

It is the spring term, and Thomas, a Year 10 pupil, is settling into the first year of his GCSEs. Over the last few weeks, Thomas has been learning about coastal landscapes, specifically how landforms like headlands and bays are formed. Mr Drake, his geography teacher, has just modelled the success criteria for the written task the class are about to undertake as part of their assessment. Last week, Mr Drake set homework to help with preparation for the assessment, but Thomas didn't do it and now he is worried that he doesn't know how to go about completing the written task. Mr Drake sets the group off on the writing, so Thomas puts his hand up and asks, 'Sir, how do I start?'

Chloe is a Year 7 pupil in one of Mr Drake's geography classes who likes to be organised and spends time at home reviewing her class notes. She knows the importance of continually reflecting on what she has learned in lessons to ensure that she does well in her exams. Chloe is self-motivated and recognises that she needs to work hard to be successful. Prior to her lesson with Mr Drake, she reviewed her previous assessment on river landscapes where she had to write a paragraph on the formation of a meander. She appreciates that this assessment will be testing the same application of knowledge, so she revisited what she did well and the feedback Mr Drake gave her to improve next time. She thinks to herself, 'I must remember this time to clearly explain how the physical processes cause the formation of the landform.' Mr Drake sets the pupils off, and Chloe starts writing her response with confidence.

In our classrooms, we would all ideally want to be teaching pupils like Chloe who are self-motivated and invest time in reviewing and reflecting on their work to identify their own strengths and weaknesses. The more our pupils can do this independently, the greater the prospect that they will be able to master our subjects and be successful. Inevitably, it takes time and conscious effort for pupils to be able to think metacognitively like Chloe and to self-regulate their own learning. It isn't something that our pupils will be able to just do by themselves overnight, and some pupils won't always believe that metacognitive strategies will benefit their learning. Our role is to educate, equip and support our pupils to behave metacognitively over time, so enabling them to build habits of self-regulation.

> **Pedagogy reflection:** Building habits of self-regulation takes time and requires teachers to deliberately model how to do this as part of their teaching.

Activity

Reflect on the scenarios of Thomas and Chloe. Try to think about two pupils in one of your classes and how they behave. Do they have scholarly habits or are they still developing them? What kind of questions do they ask you?

So, what is metacognition? Metacognition is the way pupils behave in relation to planning, monitoring and evaluating their own learning. The Education Endowment Foundation defines it as 'the ways learners monitor and purposefully direct their learning. For example, having decided that a particular cognitive strategy for memorisation is likely to be successful, a pupil then monitors whether it has indeed been successful.'[6]

Metacognition is one of the three components that underpin the concept of self-regulated learning, together with cognition and motivation:

- Cognition relates to the mental processes that take place for pupils to know, understand and learn – for example, using flash cards to promote active recall.

- Motivation relates to the desire to want to engage in metacognitive and cognitive strategies – for example, not giving up when a task is difficult and having the resilience to persevere.

The Education Endowment Foundation highlights that for pupils to behave metacognitively, they need to know and be able to use cognitive strategies and have the right motivation to keep going. This sounds relatively straightforward, but all too often pupils lack understanding about what cognitive strategies to use, as well as the motivation to keep reviewing their learning in a meaningful way. Pupils will often say:

'I don't know how to revise.'

'When I revise, it doesn't help me to learn anything.'

'I find highlighting notes works for me.'

'I get distracted by others around me.'

....

6   A. Quigley, D. Muijs and E. Stringer, *Metacognition and Self-Regulated Learning: Guidance Report* (London: Education Endowment Foundation, 2021), p. 9. Available at: https://educationendowmentfoundation.org.uk/education-evidence/guidance-reports/metacognition.

'When I do try and revise, I find it difficult and will often give up if I don't know it.'

Metacognitive strategies can be divided into three sections: plan (before), monitor (during) and evaluate (after) learning. For example, one of the biggest challenges many pupils face is knowing what they need to do first in order to start a task. You will need to consider whether the task they have been set is similar to what they have been asked to do previously in your subject. Ultimately, you want the pupils to be considering what they need to do before they begin the task, and over time to develop the confidence to be able to answer these questions for themselves. In Tom's case, it will take time for him to develop and he will need lots of opportunities for practice to reinforce how to do this in the classroom. One of the Education Endowment Foundation's key recommendations is to 'explicitly teach pupils metacognitive strategies, including how to plan, monitor, and evaluate their learning.'[7]

Here are a few examples of the types of questions that pupils should be thinking about when planning, monitoring and evaluating their learning.

When the pupils are about to undertake a task, you want them to be thinking about the following:

- How do I start?

- What should I write first?

- Have I done this type of task before?/How did I approach it last time?

When the pupils are working through the task, you want them to be thinking:

- How well am I doing?

- Am I meeting the success criteria?

---

7   Quigley et al., *Metacognition and Self-Regulated Learning*, p. 12.

- What do I need to do next?

- Who can I ask for help?

Once the pupils have finished the set task, you want them to reflect on the following:

- How well did I do?

- Did I achieve what I intended?

- What could I do better next time?

- Can I apply this elsewhere?

In the first instance, to create the conditions that enable pupils to plan, monitor and evaluate their learning, they need to know what success will look like. This is where the use of clear learning intentions and success criteria can provide the guidance they need.

In the past, I would plan a lesson by focusing on the type of activity rather than thinking about what I wanted the pupils to learn by the end of a sequence of lessons. Now, when I am planning a series of lessons, my primary focus is on what I want them to know by the end, knitted together through a core learning intention. This learning intention might take more than one lesson, but I will have a clear end goal. The next step is to consider what successfully achieving this goal will look like, and to determine what task(s) would best enable the pupils to achieve the intended outcome.

Pedagogy reflection: One clear learning intention provides clarity on what you want pupils to know by the end of a lesson sequence.

The learning intention should clearly identify what you want pupils to know by the end of the lesson or a series of lessons, not what they will need to do in order to achieve the outcome.

In essence, the learning intention should signal the knowledge and understanding you want them to acquire. For example, geography teacher Scott has been teaching his Year 10 pupils about the changes in the cross profile of a river channel. The learning intention has been presented to the pupils as: 'The cross profile of a river increases downstream from the interaction of fluvial processes.'

After the initial instruction phase of explaining, modelling, asking open and closed questions and the pupils creating notes, Scott decides to ask the pupils a question to apply the knowledge he has taught. Prior to answering a question on the reasons for the changes in the cross profile, the pupils are given the following success criteria:

SC1: Describe how the cross profile changes downstream.

SC2: Explain why fluvial processes cause change to the cross profile downstream.

SC3: Speak like a geographer throughout.

Before the pupils begin writing their answer, he gives them some time to work with a partner to reflect on how they plan to approach their answer. Peer conferencing provides pupils with a low-stakes, high-challenge opportunity to talk through their intentions before committing an answer to paper. Inner Drive observe that 'encouraging students to ask themselves better questions whilst they are learning something may be one of the most effective and efficient ways to improve their understanding of the topic.'[8]

Some examples of the types of questions Scott's pupils might ask each other in a pre-conference discussion are illustrated below:

- What are you going to talk about in your response?

- Why are you going to approach it this way?

8   Inner Drive, The Power of Self-Questioning (n.d.). Available at: https://blog.innerdrive.co.uk/the-power-of-self-questioning.

- What examples are you going to use in your response?

- Why are you going to use these examples?

- How will you use your geographical knowledge to support your response?

- How will you link your response back to the original question?

- What decision are you going to make? Why?

Alternatively, rather than getting the pupils to discuss their approach before writing, Scott could give them an opportunity to read each other's responses and then reflect on their own answer based on the original success criteria. The questions pupils might use to guide this peer post-conference are listed below:

- Reflecting on your response, did it meet the success criteria?

- How do you know you have met the success criteria?

- How might you extend your response?

- Where did you provide specific geographical evidence?

- Where have you justified your decision?

In the last fifteen years, I have found peer assessment to be one of the most difficult strategies to get right. All too often, pupils find giving feedback to their peers challenging. Many of the reasons we discussed in Chapter 2 contribute towards this problem. However, providing clear success criteria and support for these conversations gives pupils an opportunity to reflect either before they undertake independent practice or to review what they have written afterwards.

In the following case study, Poppy Gibson, a senior lecturer in education, shares her experiences of how teachers can use questioning as a reflective tool, as well as considering the benefits of e-learning platforms to support pupils to become better self-regulated learners.

Case study: Using questioning as a reflective tool with our pupils

Dr Poppy Gibson

Why are questions important? It seems relevant to start this piece with a question because questions engage and encourage the questioner to wonder and reply. Questions are valuable not only for teacher assessment of our pupils but also to inspire peer and self-assessment.

Questions also encourage us to reflect. Reflection means putting our behaviours, action and development into focus, and by being reflective, we can develop our self-awareness and strive to continue to improve our practice and build our understanding.

Working in higher education at a UK university using online platforms such as Padlet (a storyboard tool) or Mentimeter (a voting tool), questions can be posed in a way that facilitate self-assessment and knowledge evaluation. Padlet is a great way to question, as secure password-protected online 'walls' can be shared with learners to collaborate and learn socially. For example, at a recent lecture I gave on trauma, I began by sharing a Padlet with the class, simply with the title, 'What is trauma?' Beginning the session with a question encouraged everyone to reflect on their current definition of the term, and then after posting their answers onto a virtual sticky note, the pupils read the sticky notes posted by their peers. Some pupils revised their notes in response to what they read. Some pupils waited for their peers' responses to load and viewed them before contributing their own ideas. The process of self-assessment is valuable as it gives autonomy to the pupil, not only in answering the question but also in questioning their response.

Mentimeter is an excellent tech tool to use in the classroom as the anonymous feature gives many pupils the confidence to participate without the fear of being 'wrong'. Mentimeter offers a simple yet effective range of styles and themes, including word clouds, multiple choice questions, ranking answers and open-ended free text responses. I use questions in a reflective way, either at the end of sessions ('What is the most important new thing you've learned today?') or around the assessment period ('What aspect of the assignment are you still unsure about?'). While pupils join anonymously, you can see how many have taken part, and it is also easy to either screenshot the results or download them as a PDF or Excel spreadsheet after the questioning period has ended. I usually upload these results onto our virtual learning environment or email them out in our weekly newsletter to allow the pupils a further phase of collective reflection.

So, to end on a question, is questioning a powerful reflective tool? I would argue that questions are the most vital piece of our educator toolkit.

Chapter summary and reflections

- An effective process of assessing learning in schools is one of the most challenging aspects of teaching, but equally it is one of the most important ingredients for learning. How do you approach assessment in your classroom or as a leader?

- All too often, assessments are used as a tool to check teacher performance rather than how well pupils have learned the curriculum. How do you currently approach more formal assessments?

- When assessment is formative, it is assessment for learning and can be used to indicate where pupils are at and support the teacher's plans for the next steps to help their pupils improve.

- Regular low-stakes diagnostic quizzes can be used to assess what pupils have learned about the curriculum they have been taught.

- To enable pupils to plan, monitor and evaluate their learning, they need to know what success will look like. How do you explicitly present learning intentions to your pupils?

- The learning intention should make clear what you want the pupils to know by the end of the lesson or a series of lessons, not what they will need to do in order to achieve the outcome.

- Providing pupils with opportunities to reflect on their own learning allows them to self-regulate and reflect on their own strengths and areas for development. Model reflective questions with pupils so they can see how to use them to evaluate their own learning.

- Create a culture where peer assessment is used as a tool for pupils to monitor and reflect on their own learning and to see how their ideas and approaches to tasks compare with their peers.

In this chapter, we have explored how questions can be used as a tool for assessing learning to review gaps and plan the next steps in the learning process, as well as being a reflective tool to support self-regulation. In the final chapter, we will bring together all the research and summarise it in five core principles and recommendations to apply in the classroom.

Powerful Questioning : five key principles

① seq uenc ing

② framing and presenting

③ pausing

④ gathering and processing

⑤ redirecting

Chapter 5

Powerful questioning principles

Of the many techniques of teaching, questioning is by far the most commonly used at all grade levels.

William Wilen[1]

In this chapter, we will:

- Consider a core set of principles to achieve powerful questioning in the classroom.

- Explore how to plan a sequence of questions.

- Look at how to frame and present questions to pupils.

- Reflect on the role purposeful pauses have on the learning process when asking and answering questions.

- Consider what to do once we have gathered and processed question responses.

- Know how to redirect learning from the questions we have asked.

1   Wilen, *Questions, Questioning Techniques, and Effective Teaching*, p. 13.

Over the last year, spending time reading the research, reflecting on my own classroom experiences and observing teachers, I am in no doubt that questioning plays a pivotal role in classrooms. But, how can the research be applied in the everyday classroom?

Historically, there has been a great deal of focus on *why* teachers ask questions but not *how* to apply the research in the classroom. We have seen throughout the book that questions are a powerful tool to improve learning and retention in the classroom, highlighted by the numerous research studies and reflections from classroom practitioners. However, all too often the questions we ask don't activate hard thinking and instead prompt surface-level engagement between teachers and pupils. The questions asked are predominantly managerial and aim to control the day-to-day routines of our classrooms. In many cases, the flow between teachers and pupils is interrupted because the question asked is either not understood or not challenging enough.

There is a fine balance for teachers to strike when using questions, but with careful planning and deliberate practice powerful questions can reveal what pupils are thinking. In this final chapter, I will set out five core principles for using powerful questioning for knowledge retention and learning over time based around: sequencing, presenting and framing, pausing, gathering and processing, and redirecting.

The five principles provide a framework for implementing powerful questioning in your own classroom and school. By bringing together all the research, discussions with classroom practitioners and my own experiences, this final part of the book will lay out a series of recommendations for how each of the principles might work in the classroom. The various activities that have been interweaved through the chapters also provide opportunities to reflect individually and to work with colleagues to implement the use of powerful questioning.

These recommendations are based on my own interpretation of the research evidence and conversations with leading experts in the field. I have been extremely fortunate to work with the likes of John Hattie and explore his thoughts on the possibility of questions as a tool for learning and retention over time. It might be that not all the strategies or recommendations will work in your context, but I hope that the principles I have outlined will provide guidance on how to apply powerful questioning in your own classroom to promote learning retention.

First, we will return to where we started and Cotton's definition of using questions in the classroom: 'In the classroom settings, teacher questions are defined as instructional cues or stimuli that convey to students the content elements to be learned and directions for what they are to do and how they are to do it.'[2] Based on discussions in the book, we can summarise the use of questions into the four P's of purpose, process, person and point.

Purpose	Process
Questions are framed to:	Questions are presented:
▪ Check for understanding.	▪ Written.
▪ Promote knowledge recall.	▪ Verbally.
▪ Activate hard thinking.	
▪ Prompt self-regulation.	
Person	**Point**
Questions are delivered:	Questions are presented:
▪ Pupil to teacher.	▪ During lessons.
▪ Teacher to pupil.	▪ Between lessons (written).
▪ Pupil to pupil.	

2   Cotton, *Classroom Questioning*, p. 1.

Principle 1: Sequencing

Overarching recommendation: Plan out questions in a sequence to move from surface to deeper level thinking.

- Before asking questions, take time to plan out the low to higher order questions you intend to ask pupils based on a series of lessons. Aim to work with colleagues in your department to develop these questions during curriculum conversations and practise using them to build the clarity and confidence that will yield the responses you are looking for.

- Plan questions that are directly related to what is being taught, so the question provides a degree of challenge but not too much that the pupils can't answer it.

- Spend time reviewing and reflecting on the clarity of the questions asked through peer observations to support your planning and delivery of questions in lessons.

- During a lesson or series of lessons, consider using a mix of questions, both low and higher order, so they address all cognitive demands while keeping in mind the desired learning outcome. For example, begin with a series of recall questions, like 'What is …?' before moving on to questions that require a greater degree of thought, such as 'Why might …?'

- Consider pupils' prior knowledge before devising questions, taking into account how the questions you plan to ask will build on foundation knowledge. Asking higher cognitive questions straight away when introducing new knowledge is likely to decrease pupil participation due to a lack of understanding.

Transcript

In the following example, geography teacher Molly demonstrates how planning a series of questions allows her to move pupils from knowledge recall to deeper level thinking by narrowing and broadening the questions she asks.

Example 1:

Teacher:	Okay, we are going to go for hands up for this question. What is the difference between erosion and weathering?
Pupil A (Thomas):	Erosion is the wearing away of the land whereas weathering is the breakdown of rocks in situ.
Teacher:	That's correct, Thomas. Let's explore some of the processes we studied last lesson. What's hydraulic action … Valarie?
Pupil B (Valarie):	Hydraulic action is the sheer force of the water wearing away the land.
Teacher:	Excellent recall, Valarie. With the person next to you, how does hydraulic action contribute to the formation of a waterfall?

[Pupils discuss …]

Teacher: Based on what we have now discussed, how might the rate of hydraulic action vary?

Example 2:

In the second example, history teacher Rebecca uses a combination of questions in a sequence to build participation and move from low to higher order thinking.

Teacher: Who can remind me what spark caused the First World War?

[Pupil response ...]

Teacher: What has Lily done? Why is it not Emmeline Pankhurst?

[Pupil response ...]

Teacher: Lily, can you repeat what (pupil) said?

Example 3:

The final example from Silvia, a modern foreign languages subject lead, provides an illustration of how different question types can be sequenced together to probe and check for understanding.

Teacher: What tense is the sentence on the screen, Ben?

Pupil A (Ben):   It is in the past tense.

Teacher: Very good, Ben! How do we know that, Millie?

Pupil B (Millie):   Because it has got an auxiliary verb and past participle, Miss.

Teacher:	Great, Millie. And is it a regular or irregular verb, Tom?
Pupil C (Tom):	Irregular, Miss.
Teacher:	Fantastic! How do we know it is an irregular verb, Ella?
Pupil D (Ella):	Well, we build the past participle of regular verbs by adding a 'ge-' at the start of the word and a '-t' at the end. This past participle has got an '-en' at the end so it is irregular.
Teacher:	Spot on, Ella! Can you change the sentence from first-person singular to third-person singular, Gary?

[Pupil E (Gary) changes the sentence]

Teacher:	Fab! Final question: Why has Gary changed the ending on the auxiliary verb, Mia?
Pupil F (Mia):	Because the subject and the verb have to agree, Miss.

Activity 1

Create a series of questions based on a strand of your curriculum that you are planning to teach next lesson. Think about how you could ask questions that move from prompting and checking knowledge recall to encouraging deeper level thinking. Aim for four to six questions in a sequence.

Activity 2

Consider the following scenario using a sequence of questions. What could the teacher do differently to improve the question types and encourage pupils to move from surface to deeper level thinking?

Teacher: Charlie, what is the greenhouse effect?

Pupil A (Charlie): I don't know.

Teacher: Okay. Sienna, do you know what the greenhouse effect is?

Pupil B (Sienna): It's the way in which heat is trapped close to Earth's surface by greenhouse gases.

Teacher: Great. I want you all now to write down some key greenhouse gases.

Principle 2: Presenting and framing

Overarching recommendation: Deliver appropriately pitched questions that prompt the right level of thinking based on the language register used.

- Distribute questions with the aim of involving as many pupils as possible during a question-and-response session by using different strategies like cold calling, hands up, choral responses and think, pair, share.

- Frontload questions to pupils by explaining what you are expecting from them to build a responsive culture in your classroom – for example, telling them that you are looking for a hand up/hands down or a class vote before asking the question.

- Align pupil attention when presenting your questions to ensure everyone is listening and has understood the question asked.

- When asking questions, consider the tone, so the question is well presented and invites pupils to participate with a response.

- When presenting a question during a class discussion, repeat the question you have asked before giving pupils time to respond or ask several pupils to repeat the question back to you before gathering responses.

- For higher cognitive questions used with application tasks, spend some time unravelling the command of the question and what success would look like before the pupils begin independent practice.

- Avoid asking too many questions at once to avoid overloading pupils' working memory and causing cognitive overload.

- When asking pupils a question, consider the demand so that it provides the right level of challenge for the pupil.

Pedagogy reflection: Checking that pupils are paying attention when presenting a question is key to them understanding and being able to attempt to answer the question asked.

Principle 3: Pausing

Overarching recommendation: Deliver questions that allow space for pupils to receive and process the question asked.

░ Teachers should demonstrate what wait time means by live modelling to pupils during class discussions. For example, when a pupil asks a question, pause before giving a response. This will encourage them to appreciate why pausing between asking and answering a question can help to address non-explanatory responses, and to see the process in action.

░ The research indicates that there is not a set amount of time that should be provided to pupils when asking a question and expecting a response. However, it does indicates that the quality of a response increases when wait time is three seconds or more.[3] With this in mind, teachers should judge whether the pupil will need a shorter or longer time to

3   See Rowe, Wait Time.

respond based on the type of question asked. When asking a pupil a more cognitively demanding question, provide a longer wait time in comparison to asking a knowledge recall question.

- Expecting a fast response with limited wait time is likely to reduce pupil participation and increase non-explanatory responses. If you want pupils to think before answering, you need to give them the time to do so.

- During question–response sessions, teach pupils how to actively listen to others' contributions by tracking the speaker. Make it clear that you will be checking they have been actively listening after this pause phase.

Pedagogy reflection: Give pupils plenty of time to engage in active thinking to increase the probability of meaningful participation.

Activity

Work with a colleague to practise providing wait time in the context of asking a question and giving pupils time to share their response. Spend a few weeks working together to watch each other on this specific strategy for delivering questions. Share feedback and how you might improve your use of wait time to build pupil participation. Working with colleagues can build relationships that promote deliberate practice that is supportive rather than judgemental.

Principle 4: Gathering and processing

Overarching recommendation: Field questions from a range of pupils and take time to process the information gathered.

- Use a mix of questioning strategies to field questions and gather responses from pupils, and be strategic about to whom you ask questions to encourage classroom participation. Remind pupils of the role that oral responses play in the learning process.

- When cold calling, assemble responses from a selection of pupils to enable as many to contribute as possible, to check for understanding and to build a culture where answering and asking questions is part of the learning process.

- When using think, pair, share, give pupils time to think before sharing their ideas with their peers, and model with pupils how to actively listen to their peers when sharing responses.

- Use precise praise when pupils provide an answer to build their self-confidence and increase participation.

- Develop a culture where non-explanatory responses are unacceptable and pupils are encouraged to provide a full answer.

Principle 5: Redirecting

Overarching recommendation: Take time to consider how to move the learning forward after asking a question and receiving a response from pupil(s).

- If a pupil struggles to answer a question, redirect it to another pupil and then return to the original pupil to either clarify or expand on the initial question. Provide a prompt to pupils like, 'Take a moment to think back to what we learned last lesson ...'

- After asking a series of questions and gathering responses, use this as an opportunity to review the information discussed and redirect questions back to pupils who may have recalled knowledge inaccurately in the first instance. For example, 'Based on what X has just said, what have you heard?'

- When using diagnostic quizzes as part of an assessment for learning model, look for common errors across a teaching group and revisit these in subsequent lessons as part of your daily review or for reteaching a component of the curriculum.

In the closing case study, Haili Hughes, a senior lecturer and head of education at IRIS Connect, provides an insight into how you might use funnelling questions when working with a teacher to support them in their professional development – in particular, on developing their use of questions. The various activities throughout the book have provided opportunities for trialling the different strategies discussed. The case study highlights how you might use questions as a follow-up.

Case study: Using funnel questioning to support professional development for trainee teachers

Haili Hughes

The job of a teacher mentor is to guide their trainees or early career teachers (ECTs) to reflect on their own areas of development, not to tell them the answers. Of course, there are times when mentors need to use their expertise to point their mentees in the right direction, especially if they are struggling to hone the granular area they need to improve. This is the situation I found myself in last year, when my trainee was failing to focus on the specifics and which part of her pedagogy would yield the most incremental gains. After observations, I would have a clear picture of which standards and areas of the core content framework she was struggling to master, but when I attempted to draw reflective observations from her, she was often very general and couldn't pin down the target enough. I came across some research on funnel questions and decided to trial the strategy.

The funnel questioning technique has long been used in policing and social work. It is a form of questioning which is used to put those being questioned at ease, as well as probing them for as many relevant details and specifics as possible. Funnel questioning gives us a useful visual reference for thinking about our questioning skills as mentors and provides a framework that can be used practically to encourage our mentees to probe more deeply into a problem or issue with their teaching.

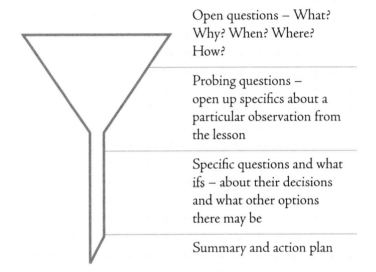

Open questions – What? Why? When? Where? How?

Probing questions – open up specifics about a particular observation from the lesson

Specific questions and what ifs – about their decisions and what other options there may be

Summary and action plan

Funnel questioning model

At the mouth of the funnel, you begin with an open question which gives the mentee the widest possible scope for responding. If they are unable to answer the question, it can be useful to repeat or rephrase to give them more reflection time. This was great for my mentee, as she was naturally quite shy and always felt nervous after being observed. By asking her an open question, she had the opportunity to talk more broadly about the lesson and her feelings about what had improved in her practice, as well as what she wished had gone differently. Some trainees/ECTs may view this as being safer as they do not have to start by drilling down into specifics.

Working down the narrowing body of the funnel, you use a series of more probing questions, where you try to draw out detailed information about a particular teaching technique or observation from the lesson. This might be something as simple as asking your mentee to provide an example to help you understand what their answer was to the previous question. This is then built on by specific questions and what ifs. For these questions, the mentor really needs to focus on particular examples and to guide the mentee to reflect on the choices they made and the rationale behind it. Part of this process will also include consideration of what other strategies or techniques they could use next time to improve.

At the bottom of the funnel, the mentor should encourage the mentee to clarify their thinking and provide a short summary of what the action plan is going forwards.

When I first used the funnel questioning model with my trainee, I was keen to get her to reflect on the level of challenge in her lessons. I wanted her to see that the hands-up approach to questioning was enabling some of the class to disengage and switch off. The question sequence went like this:

We spoke about challenge last week in our meeting. What do you think the level of challenge was like in your lesson? *(open)*

What did you do to prepare for the lesson? *(probing)*

So, how do you think that worked out? *(probing)*

Can you remember what type of questions you were
asking and which pupils answered them? *(specifics)*

What about ___ specifically? He didn't volunteer to
answer any questions. *(specifics)*

What might you have done to make sure everybody was
involved and engaged? *(what ifs)*

So, let me see if I've followed you ... *(summary)*

In your observation next week then, what could you do
differently in terms of questioning? *(action plan)*

After an initial open-ended question, my trainee had begun
to open up and the reminder of what we had previously discussed steered her in the right direction for her reflections.
I then narrowed the funnel by asking for specific examples
about how she had prepared for the lesson with this focus in
mind. The point of these questions is to work towards particular information, which is why I homed in on an individual
pupil, as it made the conversations more tangible and rooted
in the observation lesson. I also narrowed my language here
by using words that suggested I was looking for very detailed
information, such as 'specifically'.

The strategy worked well. It not only calmed my trainee and
increased her confidence, but it also helped her to relive the

lesson, gradually focusing in on the precise details, so that she could identify a granular target for herself to focus on improving in the next week.

Haili's case study provides guidance on how we can use questions to support feedback to teachers after a lesson. When we work with teachers, the quality of the discussion we have is important in building a positive experience where professional development is not being done to a colleague. The use of funnel questions allows for the feedback to be specific and the discussion to be more collaborative, leading to an action plan that will make the next steps achievable.

Concluding thoughts

This book started with the premise that questions are the heart-beat of the classroom and teachers are the blood that keeps the heart beating, the professional question-askers. Teachers are constantly asking questions, so much so that this averages at hundreds of questions every day and millions over a career – to check for understanding, to prompt self-reflection, to nudge routines, to boost confidence in oral contributions. Questions are a multifaceted pedagogy with the power to recall knowledge, challenge initial thoughts and generate curiosity to want to know more. These interactions are happening frequently and swiftly, with exchanges occurring between teachers and pupils as well as pupils to pupils. Questions are a versatile tool that drives communication in our classrooms.

The quality of the questions teachers ask plays a significant part in either promoting or hindering pupils' thinking and, in turn, the degree to which they learn. When teachers ask the right questions, it can initiate lightbulb moments that drive mutual learning for both pupils and teachers. Consequently, this form of communication dominates classrooms. Without asking questions, we are essentially guessing what our pupils know and have learned after being taught components of our curriculums. When left in the dark, learning and retention are impeded over time. Therefore, questions are an essential tool for initiating thought and unlocking opportunities for responsive teaching.

However, as illustrated by the research and the reflections from my own and others' experiences, the art of asking powerful questions is complex, with the impact dependent on how teachers execute them in the classroom. All too often, the execution leads to questions that don't serve the purpose of encouraging pupils to think. This is because the typology of the questions we ask has a big influence on the degree to which we encourage pupils to think at a surface or deeper level. As we have explored, a number of research studies have indicated that teachers ask more managerial and lower tariff knowledge recall questions. Whether we promote surface or deeper level thinking will be determined by the instructional goal of the questions we propose. As we have seen, there will be times when managerial questions are required to nudge classroom norms and redirect pupils with their behaviour.

I hope this book provides sufficient guidance to support the use of powerful questioning in your classroom and wider school environment. Through the careful implementation of the strategies outlined, you can create the conditions that will promote learning and retention over time.

Bibliography

Abdullah, M. Y., Bakar, N. R. A. and Mahbob, M. H. (2012). Student's Participation in Classroom: What Motivates Them to Speak Up?, *Procedia – Social and Behavioral Sciences*, 51: 516–522. Available at: https://doi.org/10.1016/j.sbspro.2012.08.199.

Alfke, D. (1974). Asking Operational Questions: A Basic Skill for Science Inquiry, *Science and Children*, 11(17), 18–19.

Ausubel, D. P. (1978). *Educational Psychology: A Cognitive View* (New York: Holt, Rinehart & Winston).

Barell, J. (2003). *Developing More Curious Minds* (Alexandria, VA: Association for Supervision and Curriculum Development).

Berger, W. (2014). *A More Beautiful Question: The Power of Inquiry* (New York: Bloomsbury).

Birbili, M. (2017). *Supporting Young Children to Ask Productive Questions* (Research in Practice) (Watson, ACT: Early Childhood Australia).

Black, P. and Wiliam, D. (1998). *Inside the Black Box: Raising Standards Through Classroom Assessment* (London: GL Assessment).

Bloom, B., Englehart, M., Furst, E., Hill, W. and Krathwohl, D. (1956). *Taxonomy of Educational Objectives: The Classification of Educational Goals. Handbook I: Cognitive Domain* (New York and Toronto: Longmans, Green).

Blosser, P. E. (1991). *How to … Ask the Right Questions* (Washington, DC: National Science Teachers Association).

Briggs, S. (2020). The Importance of Kids Asking Questions, *informED* (25 March). Available at: https://www.opencolleges.edu.au/informed/features/importance-kids-asking-questions.

Britton, J. (1983). Writing and the Story of the World. In B. M. Kroll and C. G. Wells (eds), *Explorations in the Development of Writing: Theory, Research, and Practice* (New York: Wiley), pp. 3–30.

Brown, G. A. and Edmondson, R. (1989). Asking Questions. In E. C. Wragg (ed.), *Classroom Teaching Skills* (London: Routledge), pp. 97–120.

Brualdi Timmins, A. C. (1998). Classroom Questions, *Practical Assessment, Research, and Evaluation*, vol. 6, article 6. Available at: https://doi.org/10.7275/05rc-jd18.

Chin, C. (2002). Student-Generated Questions: Encouraging Inquisitive Minds in Learning Science, *Teaching and Learning*, 23(1), 59–67. Available at: https://repository.nie.edu.sg/bitstream/10497/292/1/TL-23-1-59.pdf.

Chouinard, M. M. (2007). Children's Questions: A Mechanism for Cognitive Development, *Monographs of the Society for Research in Child Development*, 72(1): vii–ix, 1–112; discussion 113–126. https://doi.org/10.1111/j.1540-5834.2007.00412.x

Clear, J. (2018). *Atomic Habits: An Easy & Proven Way to Build Good Habits & Break Bad Ones* (London: Random House Business).

Cotton, K. (2001). *Classroom Questioning* (School Improvement Research Series) (Portland, OR: North West Regional Educational Laboratory). Available at: https://educationnorthwest.org/sites/default/files/ClassroomQuestioning.pdf.

Dantonio, M. (1990). *How Can We Create Thinkers? Questioning Strategies That Work for Teachers* (Bloomington, IN: National Education Service).

Elsworthy, E. (2017). Curious Children Ask 73 Questions Each Day – Many of Which Parents Can't Answer, Says Study. *The Independent* (3 December). Available at: https://www.independent.co.uk/news/uk/home-news/curious-children-questions-parenting-mum-dad-google-answers-inquisitive-argos-toddlers-chad-valley-tots-town-a8089821.html.

Engel, S. (2021). Many Kids Ask Fewer Questions When They Start School. Here's How We Can Foster Their Curiosity, *Time* (23 February). Available at: https://time.com/5941608/schools-questions-fostering-curiousity.

Filippone, M. (1998). Questioning at the Elementary Level. Unpublished MA dissertation, Kean University, NJ. Available at: https://eric.ed.gov/?id=ED417431.

Fisher, D. and Frey, N. (2014). *Checking for Understanding: Formative Assessment Techniques for Your Classroom*, 2nd edn (Alexandria, VA: Association for Supervision and Curriculum Development).

Fletcher-Wood, H. (2018). *Responsive Teaching: Cognitive Science and Formative Assessment in Practice* (Abingdon and New York: Routledge).

Frazier, B. N., Gelman, S. A. and Wellman, H. M. (2016). Young Children Prefer and Remember Satisfying Explanations, *Journal of Cognition and Development*, 17(5), 718–736. https://doi.org/10.1080/15248372.2015.1098649

Gall, M. D. (1970). The Use of Questions in Teaching, *Review of Educational Research*, 40(5), 707–721. https://doi.org/10.3102/00346543040005707

Gall, M. D. (1984). Synthesis of Research on Teachers' Questioning, *Educational Leadership*, 42(3), 40–47.

Gall, M. D., Ward, B. A., Berliner, D. C., Cahen, L. S., Winne, P. H., Elashoff, J. D. and Stanton, G. C. (1978). Effects of Questioning Techniques and Recitation on Student Learning, *American Educational Research Journal*, 15, 175–199.

Gandhi, I. (1975). *Speeches and Writings* (New York: Harper & Row).

Geary, D. C. (2004). *The Origin of Mind: Evolution of Brain, Cognition, and General Intelligence* (Washington, DC: American Psychological Association).

Glenz, T. (2014). The Importance of Learning Students' Names, *Journal on Best Teaching Practices*, 21–22. Available at: http://teachingonpurpose.org/wp-content/uploads/2015/03/Glenz-T.-2014.-The-importance-of-learning-students-names.pdf.

Glišić, T. Č. (2017). Why Do Children Ask Questions: New Classification of Preschool Children's Questions, *Teaching Innovations*, 30(2): 114–127. Available at: http://www.inovacijeunastavi.rs/wp-content/uploads/Inovacije2-17en/PR08.pdf.

Hall, M. (2015). A Guide to Bloom's Taxonomy, *The Innovative Instructor Blog* (30 January). Available at: https://ii.library.jhu.edu/2015/01/30/a-guide-to-blooms-taxonomy.

Hanna, G. P. (1977). The Effect of Wait Time on the Quality of Response of First-Grade Children. Unpublished master's thesis, University of Kansas, KS.

Hindman, A. H., Wasik, B. A. and Bradley, D. (2018). The Question Is Just the Beginning: How Head Start Teachers Use Wait Time and Feedback During Book Reading. Paper presented at the annual meeting of the American Educational Research Association, New York, April.

Inner Drive (n.d.). The Power of Self-Questioning. Available at: https://blog.innerdrive.co.uk/the-power-of-self-questioning.

Johnston, J. H., Markle, G. C. and Hayley-Oliphant, A. (1987). What Research Says About Questioning in the Classroom, *Middle School Journal*, 18(4), 29–33. https://doi.org/10.1080/00940771.1987.114 94749

Jones, K. and Wiliam, D. (2021). Getting the 'Think-Pair-Share' Technique Right, *ASCD Blog* (13 October). Available at: https:// www.ascd.org/blogs/getting-the-think-pair-share-technique-right.

Lemov, D. (2021). *Teach Like a Champion 3.0: 63 Techniques That Put Students on the Path to College*, 3rd edn (San Francisco, CA: Jossey-Bass).

Lemov, D. and Jones, K. (2021). On Hybrid Question Design in Retrieval Practice, *Teach Like a Champion* (14 September). Available at: https://teachlikeachampion.org/blog/ on-hybrid-question-design-in-retrieval-practice-with-kate-jones.

Leven, T. and Long, R. (1981). *Effective Instruction* (Washington, DC: Association for Supervision and Curriculum Development).

Liu, J. (2001). *Asian Students Classroom Communication Patterns in US Universities: An Emic Perspective* (Westport, CT: Greenwood Publishing).

Losada, M. and Heaphy, E. (2004). The Role of Positivity and Connectivity in the Performance of Business Teams: A Nonlinear Dynamics Model, *American Behavioral Scientist*, 47(6), 740–765. https://doi.org/10.1177/0002764203260

Lyman, F. (1987). Think-Pair-Share: An Ending Teaching Technique, *MAA-CIE Cooperative News*, 1, 1–2.

Lynch, M. (2018). 10 Common Questions Kids Ask and How You Should Answer, *The Edvocate* (25 October). Available at: https:// www.theedadvocate.org/10-common-questions-kids-ask-answer.

McLeod, S. A. (2013). Stages of Memory: Encoding Storage and Retrieval, *Simply Psychology* (5 August). Available at: https://www. simplypsychology.org/memory.html.

Mehan, H. (1979). *Learning Lessons: Social Organization in the Classroom* (Cambridge, MA: Harvard University Press).

Miller, G. A. (1956). The Magical Number Seven, Plus or Minus Two: Some Limits On Our Capacity for Processing Information, *Psychological Review*, 63(2), 81–97. https://doi.org/10.1037/ h0043158

Morgan, N. and Saxton, J. (1991). *Teaching, Questioning and Learning* (London: Routledge).

Mustapha, S. M., Rahman, N. S. N. A. and Yunus, M. M. (2010). Factors Influencing Classroom Participation: A Case Study of Malaysian Undergraduate Students, *Procedia Social and Behavioral Sciences*, 9, 1079–1084. https://doi.org/10.1016/j.sbspro.2010.12.289

Myatt, M. (2022). Overrated: – Content coverage aka 'Jackson Pollocking the curriculum' Underrated: – Concepts aka big ideas, *Twitter* (27 July, 9.54am). Available at: https://twitter.com/MaryMyatt/status/1552215754526920710?s=20&t=6NMIdqwMSlTDNe0dbY7hrQ.

Olalekan, A. B. (2016). Influence of Peer Group Relationship on the Academic Performance of Students in Secondary Schools: A Case Study of Selected Secondary Schools in Atiba Local Government Area of Oyo State, *Global Journal of Human-Social Science*, 16(A4), 37–40.

Orletsky, S. (1997). *Questioning and Understanding to Improve Learning and Thinking (QUILT): The Evaluation Results* (Charleston, WV: Appalachia Educational Laboratory). Available at: https://eric.ed.gov/?id=ED403230.

Orlich, D. C., Harder, R. J., Callahan, R. C., Trevisan, M. S. and Brown, A. H. (2010). *Teaching Strategies: A Guide to Effective Instruction* (Boston, MA: Wadsworth Cengage Learning).

Piaget, J. (1952) *The Origins of Intelligence in Children*, tr. M. T. Cook (New York: International Universities Press).

Popham, W. J. (2007) All About Accountability: The Lowdown on Learning Progressions, *EL*, 64(7). Available at: https://www.ascd.org/el/articles/the-lowdown-on-learning-progressions.

Pressley, M. (1992). Beyond Direct Explanation: Transactional Instruction of Reading Comprehension Strategies, *Elementary School Journal*, 92(5), 513–555. https://doi.org/10.1086/461705

Quigley, A., Muijs, D. and Stringer, E. (2021). *Metacognition and Self-Regulated Learning: Guidance Report* (London: Education Endowment Foundation). Available at: https://educationendowmentfoundation.org.uk/education-evidence/guidance-reports/metacognition.

Raba, A. A. A. (2017). The Influence of Think-Pair-Share (TPS) on Improving Students' Oral Communication Skills in EFL Classrooms, *Creative Education*, 8(1), 12–23. Available at: https://www.scirp.org/journal/paperinformation.aspx?paperid=73454.

Renkl, A. (2014). Toward An Instructionally Oriented Theory of Example-Based Learning, *Cognitive Science*, 38(1), 1–37. https://doi.org/10.1111/cogs.12086

Rosenshine, B. (2012). Principles of Instruction: Research-Based Strategies That All Teachers Should Know, *American Educator* (spring), 12–19. Available at: https://www.aft.org/sites/default/files/Rosenshine.pdf.

Rowe, M. B. (1986). Wait Time: Slowing Down May Be a Way of Speeding Up!, *Journal of Teacher Education*, 37(1), 43–50. https://doi.org/10.1177/002248718603700110

Schmoker, M. (2006). *Results Now: How We Can Achieve Unprecedented Improvements in Teaching and Learning* (Alexandria, VA: Association for Supervision and Curriculum Development).

Schunk, D. H. and Pajares, F. (2002). The Development of Academic Self-Efficacy. In A. Wigfield and J. Eccles (eds), *Development of Achievement Motivation* (San Diego, CA: Academic Press), pp. 15–31.

Severns, M. (2009). Why Ask Why? New Research Looks at Children's Questions, *New America* (30 November). Available at: https://www.newamerica.org/education-policy/early-elementary-education-policy/early-ed-watch/why-ask-why-new-research-looks-at-childrens-questions.

Sherrington, T. and Claviglioli, O. (2020). *Teaching WalkThrus: Five-Step Guides to Instructional Coaching, Vol. 1* (Woodbridge: John Catt Educational).

Stahl, R. J. (1994). Using 'Think-Time' and 'Wait-Time' Skillfully in the Classroom, *ERIC Digest*. Available at: https://files.eric.ed.gov/fulltext/ED370885.pdf.

Sutton, J. (2020). Socratic Questioning in Psychology: Examples and Techniques, *Positive Psychology* (19 June). Available at: https://positivepsychology.com/socratic-questioning.

Suydam, M. N. (1985). Research Report: Questions?, *Arithmetic Teacher*, 32(6), 18.

Sweller, J. (2021). *Why Inquiry-Based Approaches Harm Students' Learning*. Centre of Independent Studies Analysis Paper 24 (August). Available at: https://www.cis.org.au/wp-content/uploads/2021/08/ap24.pdf.

Taba, H. (1966). *Teaching Strategies and Cognitive Functioning in Elementary School Children*. Cooperative Research Project No. 2404

(San Francisco, CA: San Francisco State College). Available at: https://files.eric.ed.gov/fulltext/ED025448.pdf.

Takayoshi, P. and Van Ittersum, D. (2018). Wait Time: Making Space for Authentic Learning, *Kent State University Center for Teaching and Learning*. Available at: https://www.kent.edu/ctl/wait-time-making-space-authentic-learning.

Tamar, L. and Long, R. (1981). *Effective Instruction* (Alexandria, VA: Association for Supervision and Curriculum Development). Available at: https://files.eric.ed.gov/fulltext/ED200572.pdf.

Tofade, T., Elsner, J. and Haines, S. T. (2013). Best Practice Strategies for Effective Use of Questions as a Teaching Tool, *American Journal of Pharmaceutical Education*, 77(7), article 155. Available at: https://www.ncbi.nlm.nih.gov/pmc/articles/PMC3776909.

van Zee, E. and Minstrell, J. (1997). Using Questioning to Guide Student Thinking, *Journal of the Learning Sciences*, 6(2), 227–269. https://doi.org/10.1207/s15327809jls0602_3

Vogt, E. E., Brown, J. and Isaacs, D. (2003). *The Art of Powerful Questions: Catalyzing Insight, Innovation, and Action* (Mill Valley, CA: Whole Systems Associates).

Vosniadou, S., Ioannides, C., Dimitrakopoulou, A. and Papademetriou, E. (2001). Designing Learning Environments to Promote Conceptual Change in Science, *Learning and Instruction*, 11(4–5), 381–419. https://doi.org/10.1016/S0959-4752(00)00038-4

Wilen, W. W. (ed.) (1987). *Questions, Questioning Techniques, and Effective Teaching* (Washington, DC: National Education Association). Available at: https://files.eric.ed.gov/fulltext/ED310102.pdf.

Wimer, J. W., Ridenour, C. S., Thomas, K. and Place, A. W. (2001). Higher Order Teacher Questioning of Boys and Girls in Elementary Mathematics Classrooms, *Journal of Educational Research*, 95(2), 84–92. https://doi.org/10.1080/00220670109596576

Wong, H. and Wong, R. (2018). *The First Days of School: How To Be An Effective Teacher* (Mountain View, CA: Harry K. Wong Publications).

Wragg, E. C. (1993). *Primary Teaching Skills* (London: Routledge).

Wragg, E. C. and Brown, G. (2001). *Questioning in the Secondary School* (Successful Teaching Series) (Abingdon and New York: Routledge).

The CPD Curriculum
Creating conditions for growth
Zoe Enser and Mark Enser
ISBN: 978-178583569-8

Shares expert and practical guidance for schools on designing and delivering continuing professional development (CPD) that truly lives up to its name.

There is a wealth of research available on professional learning, from both within and outside the education sphere, and in this book Zoe and Mark pull it all together to help school leaders optimise teachers' ongoing learning and growth.

Zoe and Mark explain how schools can overcome issues with CPD that can leave teachers plateauing in their development after just a few years, and share a variety of case studies that illustrate the key components of an effective CPD programme that builds on teachers' prior knowledge.

The authors spell out the importance of CPD and explain how, when done well, it gives teachers the agency to make professional decisions informed by the best evidence and experience they have to hand. Furthermore, they explore how high-quality professional development contributes not only to a collaborative culture within the school staff team and enhanced job satisfaction for teachers, but also to improved student outcomes.

Suitable for school leaders, heads of department and CPD leads in all settings.

Teach Like Nobody's Watching
The essential guide to effective and efficient teaching
Mark Enser
ISBN: 978-178583399-1

Sets out a time-efficient approach to teaching that will reduce teachers' workload and enhance their pupils' levels of engagement and attainment.

At a time when schools are crying out for more autonomy and trust, teacher and bestselling author Mark Enser asks educators the critical question 'How would you teach if nobody were watching?' and empowers them with the tools and confidence to do just that.

Mark argues that a quality education is rooted in simplicity. In this book he convincingly strips away the layers of contradictory pedagogical advice that teachers have received over the years and lends weight to the three key pillars that underpin effective, efficient teaching: the lesson, the curriculum and the school's support structure.

Suitable for all teachers in both primary and secondary schools.

Test-Enhanced Learning
A practical guide to improving academic outcomes for all students
Kristian Still
ISBN: 978-178583658-9

An informative guidebook that explores the wealth of evidence behind and the benefits of test-enhanced learning, spaced retrieval practice and personalisation.

Detailing the most up-to-date research into improving learning and retention, it takes us on a journey into test-enhanced learning, spaced retrieval practice, motivation, metacognition and personalisation. In so doing, the book provides a blueprint for all teachers and schools to improve the academic outcomes of their students and to achieve this in ways that improve the motivation of learners and reduce the workload for teachers.

Kristian Still has been developing these ideas with his classes for many years and has achieved considerable success in terms of the direct learning gains, improved assessment grades of his pupils and the indirect gains in students growing confidence in lessons, with a wider group of pupils contributing to class and improved classroom behaviour. Consequently, students are finding greater comfort in class and experiencing less pressure or underpreparedness when a question is asked.

Suitable for all teachers in all settings.